The TOPSY TURVY *World* —*OF*— GILBERT AND SULLIVAN

To Jan and Mark —
Season's Greetings and all the
best for 2020 —

Keith.
December 2019

Left: Poster for an American production of *The Pirates of Penzance*, 1880.

Right: Frontispiece by Alice B. Woodward to *The Pinafore Picture Book*, 1908.
Ralph Rackstraw's opening aria lyric is deliberately archaic and high-flown. He's singing about a bird who is himself singing, forlorn, in the moonlight.

The
TOPSY
TURVY
World
—OF—
GILBERT AND SULLIVAN

KEITH DOCKRAY AND ALAN SUTTON

FONTHILL

Front cover image:

The Pirate Publisher—An International Burlesque that has the Longest Run on Record by Joseph Ferdinand Keppler, published as a centrefold in US magazine *Puck*, 24 February 1886. A commentary on the state of US copyright laws that, prior to a 1911 treaty, generally offered no protection to foreign authors and works.

This was a direct 'take' on *The Pirates of Penzance*, and W. S. Gilbert is one of the British authors depicted to the right.

CHORUS OF BRITISH AUTHORS:
Behold the Pirate Publisher stand,
Stealing our brains for Yankee-land;
He's rude, uncultured, bold and free—
THE PIRATE-PUBLISHER: You bet your life:
The Law—that's Me.

CHORUS OF FRENCH VICTIMS:
He takes our novels and our plays,
And never a red centime he pays;
He is more Monarque than the Grand Louis—
THE P. P.: You bet your life: The Law—that's Me.

CHORUS OF GERMAN AND OTHER SUFFERERS:
The labors of our studious brains
All go to swell his sinful gains;
He ravages Norway and Germanee—
THE P. P.: You bet your life: The Law—that's Me.

CHORUS OF HUMBLE AMERICAN AUTHORS:
Though no one ever, in all this fuss,
Has thought of according rights to us—
Remember we're pillaged across the sea—
THE P. P.: Who cares for them: The Law—that's Me.

www.fonthillmedia.com
office@fonthillmedia.com

First published in the United Kingdom
and the United States of America 2020

British Library Cataloguing in Publication Data:
A catalogue record for this book is available from the British Library

Copyright © Keith Dockray & Alan Sutton 2020

ISBN 978-1-78155-776-1

Typeset in Minion Pro 10.5pt on 15pt
Printed and bound in England

Preface

As a young teenager in 1957 a chance visit to an amateur performance of *Trial by Jury* in a local church hall first awakened my interest in the musical collaboration of W. S. Gilbert and Arthur Sullivan. When, soon after, I discovered the D'Oyly Carte Opera Company, I became completely hooked; over the next twenty years I saw many of its productions, often featuring the incomparable John Reed in leading comic roles; and the announcement of the original company's final performance, at London's Adelphi Theatre on 27 February 1982, certainly came as a very considerable and unwelcome shock. Meanwhile, a few years earlier in 1977, I had myself put together a two-hour entertainment, *The Topsy Turvy World of Gilbert and Sullivan*, for an Open University summer school at the University of York. Towards the end of my years teaching at Huddersfield Polytechnic/University, in 1994, I reprised it, this time in a conference room above a town centre pub. Then, a decade later in 2004, I revived it for a final time at the University of the West of England: my last ever public performance! Now, more than forty years after its first airing, what amounted to a two-hour lecture (with D'Oyly Carte recordings by way of musical accompaniment) has provided most of the text for this booklet. Illustrations and captions have been compiled by Alan Sutton as part of this, our third, collaborative venture: the others were *Henry VIII* (2016) and *Politics, Society and Homosexuality in Post-War Britain* (2017). Completion of the trilogy, indeed, marks the culmination of a personal/ professional friendship that has lasted four decades.

Keith Dockray
Bristol
July 2019

Left: Performers in a contemporary performance of *The Pirates of Penzance*; a studio photograph.

Right: Richard D'Oyly Carte, photographed in New York, *c.* 1878, by Mora, of 707, Broadway.

Contents

Prologue

Many years ago there was an entertaining programme on BBC Radio 4 called *The Year in Question*. It always began the same way. A distinguished panel was called upon to identify a particular year from snippets of information about it. 1875 would certainly have provided a good 'year in question'. Disraeli and the Conservative party were in power, having taken over from Gladstone and the Liberals in 1874. 1875 was a notably productive year for social legislation: for instance, there was a Trade Union Act, an Artisans' Dwellings Act, a Sale of Food and Drugs Act and a Public Health Act. It was the year, too, when Disraeli bought on the government's behalf (for £4 million) Khedive Ismail's shares in the Suez Canal Company. For any Gilbert and Sullivan enthusiast, however, 1875 has a particular significance: the first successful, influential and lasting collaboration of William Schwenk Gilbert (1836-1911) and Arthur Seymour Sullivan (1842-1900) on the one-act comic opera *Trial by Jury*.

Trial by Jury was not the first writing W. S. Gilbert had done for the stage; nor was it the first collaboration of Gilbert and Sullivan. Like those of a number of later operas, moreover, the plot of *Trial by Jury* was based on an earlier piece by Gilbert, as well as clearly drawing on the writer's own experience.

After completing a Bachelor of Arts degree at King's College London in 1856, Gilbert had decided that he must do his bit in the Crimean War. Unfortunately for him (though, perhaps, fortunately for us!) the war unexpectedly ended: as a result the exam for which he had been preparing was indefinitely postponed! A few years later, however, he did join the army volunteers, finally retiring from the Royal Aberdeenshire Highlanders in 1878 with the honorary rank of major. This experience, no doubt, produced raw material for the army officers we find in the operas, notably Major General Stanley in *The Pirates of Penzance* and Colonel Calverley in *Patience*. Also, in the late 1850s, Gilbert *did* sit a competitive examination and, on the strength of it, obtained an assistant clerkship in the education department of the Privy Council Office. Thereafter, he spent some four years in what he himself later described as an 'ill-organised' and 'ill-governed office' until, on inheriting the princely sum of £300, he 'resolved to emancipate' himself from the 'detestable thraldom of this baleful office'. Still, it was all grist to the mill, and Gilbert was later to send up examinations in both *HMS Pinafore* and *Iolanthe*, as well as directing his wit at bureaucracy, notably in *The Mikado*.

With £300 in his pocket, Gilbert decided to set himself up as a barrister; he was called to the bar in 1863; and after practising in London for several years, he joined the northern circuit (albeit only briefly) in 1866. During this time he frequently attended the assizes (even making the odd appearance at the Old Bailey) but, by no stretch of the imagination, could he be regarded as successful barrister. Indeed, his very first case (the unsuccessful defence of a woman) set the scene for an *undistinguished* legal career! As he himself recollected later:

> No sooner had the learned judge pronounced sentence than the poor soul stooped down and, taking off a heavy boot, flung it at my head as a reward from my eloquence on her behalf, accompanying the assault with a torrent of invective against my abilities as a counsel and my line of defence.

Nor did the law prove financially lucrative. In his first two years at the bar Gilbert only earned £75 and, over four years of practice, he averaged just five clients a year. Nevertheless he did develop a great love of the law which remained with him for the rest of his life and, particularly in his later years, he himself became notably litigious on his own behalf. Perhaps he truly believed, as his Lord Chancellor declared in *Iolanthe*, that:

> The law is the true embodiment
> Of everything that's excellent.

Not that this prevented him from drawing on his own experiences in order to satirise the law. This is most apparent in *Trial by Jury* and *Iolanthe* but there is plenty more in *The Pirates of Penzance*, *Ruddigore* and *Utopia Limited*.

In 1861 the penny magazine *Fun* was founded and W. S. Gilbert was soon contributing a great deal of humorous material to its pages. Indeed it has rightly been emphasised, *Fun* was 'the cradle of the operas; Gilbert wrote poems, parodies and articles for it over many years'; and, when seeking inspiration for his librettos, he frequently went back to his earlier work. His first play, *Uncle Baby*, was staged in 1863, while his first burlesque, glorying in the title *Dulcamara* or *The Little Duck and the Great Quack*, was first performed at the St James's Theatre, London, on 29 December 1866. Of this travesty of Donizetti's opera *L'elisir d'amore*, Gilbert himself later remarked:

> The piece, written in ten days and rehearsed in a week, met with much more success than it deserved.

He was certainly right! Nevertheless not only did it run for several months, it was also twice revived as well. A whole series of other burlesques followed, again often sporting equally idiotic titles: *The Merry Zingara or The Tipsy Gypsy and the Pipsy Wipsy* (Royalty Theatre, London, 21 March 1868), for instance, and *Robert the Devil or The Nun, the Dun and the Son of a Gun* (Gaiety Theatre, London, 21 December 1868). In 1869 he published *The Bab Ballads*, another major source for his later librettos; he wrote a number of verse-plays over the years, one of which (*The Princess*, staged in 1870) was to provide the foundation of his comic opera *Princess Ida*; and, in addition, he penned a series of dramatic sketches, several of which were set to music by Frederic Clay. More importantly, or so he recollected years later, it was Clay who, in 1871, introduced him to the young composer Arthur Sullivan.

By 1871 Sullivan, like his soon-to-be collaborator in comic opera, had also begun to make a reputation for himself. As a boy, so he recalled years later, he 'learned to play every wind instrument, with which I formed not merely a passing acquaintance but a real lifelong intimate friendship'. He mastered the piano as well and won a scholarship to the Royal Academy of Music where, before long, he became thoroughly hooked on composition. A suite of incidental music to William Shakespeare's *The Tempest*, performed in London in April 1862, received a near rave review in *The Athenaeum*:

> Years on years have elapsed since we heard a work by so young an artist so full of promise, so full of fancy, showing so much conscientiousness.

Sullivan himself later recalled that even Charles Dickens, on hearing a performance of the suite, not only 'seized my hand with his iron grip' but also declared 'I don't pretend to know much about music but I do know that I have been listening to a very great work'. At this time Sullivan was just twenty years old! Over the ensuing years further serious compositions followed, including a short ballet (1864), a cello concerto (1866) and a couple of overtures (1866 and 1867). Hints of a less serious musical future also emerged in 1867, however, when he wrote the music and F. C. Burnand the libretto for a short light-hearted Offenbach-inspired operetta *Cox and Box*. And, maybe he even met W. S. Gilbert as early as 1869.

Gilbert and Sullivan first worked together on a burlesque entitled *Thespis*, staged at the Gaiety Theatre on 26 December 1871, and clocking up just 63 performances in all. Sadly, although Gilbert's text survives, most of the musical score has vanished. Nor did *Thespis* establish the Gilbert and Sullivan partnership. The two went their separate ways once more until, in 1875, Richard D'Oyly Carte brought them together again: the result, this time, was the much more successful one-act comic opera *Trial by Jury* (first of 131 performances, at the Royalty Theatre where D'Oyly Carte was general manager, 25 March 1875). Soon afterwards Carte formed his own comedy opera production company; a few years later he built the Savoy Theatre; and, most importantly, he bore prime responsibility for staging no fewer than twelve full-length Gilbert and Sullivan comic operas between 1877 and 1896:

The Sorcerer	(17 November 1877, 178 performances)
HMS Pinafore	(25 May 1878, 571 performances)
The Pirates of Penzance	(31 December 1879, New York, 3 April 1880, London, 363 performances)
Patience	(23 April 1881, 578 performances)
Iolanthe	(25 November 1882, 398 performances)
Princess Ida	(5 January 1884, 246 performances)
The Mikado	(14 March 1885, 672 performances)
Ruddigore	(22 January 1887, 288 performances)
The Yeomen of the Guard	(30 October 1888, 423 performances)
The Gondoliers	(7 December 1889, 544 performances)
Utopia Limited	(7 October 1893, 245 performances)
The Grand Duke	(7 March 1896,123 performances)

Not only are the plots of virtually all these comic operas ingenious, the lyrics witty and the music compelling, they also present modern audiences with splendidly rich and satirical evocations of Victorian England and its society.

*Victorian England
in the Savoy Operas*

1

Law and the Legal Scene

Clearly, W. S. Gilbert had a particular interest in, and enthusiasm for, the law: indeed, of all the components of later nineteenth-century English life that figure in the operas, the legal scene is most frequently and most thoroughly explored.

In the 1860s, when Gilbert was failing to make a good living for himself at the bar, the law itself left a good deal to be desired. There was certainly plenty for him to get his teeth into and he drew very much on his own experiences. In *Utopia Limited*, for instance, we have a splendid description of a barrister, Sir Bailey Barr, QC, MP:

> A complicated gentleman allow me to present,
> Of all the arts and sciences the terse embodiment.
> He's a great arithmetician who can demonstrate with ease
> That two and two are three or five or anything you please.
> An eminent logician who can make it clear to you
> That black is white when looked at from the proper point of view;
> A marvellous philologist who'll undertake to show
> That 'yes' is but another and a neater form of 'no'.
> All preconceived ideas on any subject I can scout,
> And demonstrate beyond all possibility of doubt,
> That whether you're an honest man or whether you're a thief,
> Depends on whose solicitor has given me my brief.

In *Patience* it is the solicitor who has to raffle the poet Reginald Bunthorne among 'twenty love-sick maidens'; there is a notary in *The Sorcerer*; and plenty of legal stuff can be found in *Ruddigore* as well. There is a good deal, too, in *The Mikado*. Thus, for instance, in KoKo's 'little list' of those who 'never would be missed', there is a joke-cracking judge:

… that *Nisi Prius* nuisance, who just now is rather rife,
The judicial humourist—I've got *him* on the list!

Then there is the Mikado's own song:

My object all sublime
I shall achieve in time—
To let the punishment fit the crime.

And, in *Utopia Limited*, King Paramount, looking for a punishment to fit a particular case, declares:

I am in constant touch with
the Mikado of Japan, who is
a leading authority on such
points.

The police in *The Pirates of Penzance* may be a lily-livered lot but they do see themselves as upholders of the law; while, in the same opera, the daughters of Major-General Stanley (when seized by the pirates) take their stand thus:

Proceed, against our will, to wed us all,
Just bear in mind that we are Wards in Chancery,
And father is a Major-General.

And Gilbert was to return to 'Wards in Chancery' again in *Iolanthe*!

Gilbert and Sullivan's first successful collaboration, *Trial by Jury*, has an almost entirely law-orientated plot. The *scene* is a court of law: indeed, Gilbert seems to have based it on the Clerkenwell Sessions House where he himself had practised (see page 59). The *case* to be tried is an action for breach-of-promise (possibly based on the case of 'Bardell versus Pickwick'). And, in the original production, the key role of the *judge* was played by Arthur Sullivan's brother Frederic: indeed, it probably owed much of its success to his accomplished rendering of the part. Certainly Gilbert himself was to comment later:

The surprising success of *Trial by Jury* was due in no slight degree to poor Fred Sullivan's admirable performance.

Frederic himself died in January 1877 and, indeed, Sullivan's emotionally-charged 'Lost Chord' was an *In Memoriam* to him.

During the course of the trial Gilbert presents us with a romantic and broken-hearted plaintive, Angelina, a fickle and disenchanted defendant, Edwin, a judge with a distinctly roving eye, a set of singularly designing bridesmaids, and a jury rendered quite incapable of objectivity. In his opening song the usher instructs the jury to set aside all kinds of vulgar prejudice and exhorts them to approach the case with:

> … stern judicial frame of mind,
> From bias free of every kind.

Since, however, he then goes on to sympathise with the 'broken-hearted bride' and implores the jury to 'condole with her distress of mind', it is only too obvious where his sympathies lie! This is particularly clear from his remarks on the defendant:

> And when amid the plaintiff's shrieks,
> The ruffianly defendant speaks—
> Upon the other side;
> What *he* may say you needn't bide.

The arrival of the judge himself is followed, after some difficulty in achieving silence in court, by the judge' song. The first of many splendid patter-songs Gilbert was to write over the next few years, it is essentially a homily on the usefulness of marriage as a means of advancing a legal career (advice which Gilbert himself might usefully have followed in the early 1860s!):

When I, good friends, was called to the bar,
I'd an appetite fresh and hearty,
But I was, as many young barristers are,
An impecunious party.
I'd a swallow-tail coat of a beautiful blue—
A brief which I bought of a booby—
A couple of shirts and a collar or two,
And a ring that looked like a ruby!

In Westminster Hall I danced a dance,
Like a semi-despondent fury;
For I thought I should never hit on a chance
Of addressing a British jury.—
But I soon got tired of third class journeys,
And dinners of bread and water;
So I fell in love with a rich attorney's
Elderly, ugly daughter.

The rich attorney he jumped with joy,
And replied to my fond professions:
'You shall reap the reward of your pluck, my boy,
At the Bailey and Middlesex sessions.
You'll soon get used to her looks,' said he,
'And a very nice girl you'll find her!
She may very well pass for forty-three
In the dusk, with the light behind her!'

The rich attorney was good as his word;
The briefs came trooping gaily,
And every day my voice was heard
At the Sessions of Ancient Bailey.
All thieves who could my fees afford
Relied on my orations,
And many a burglar I've restored
To his friends and his relations.

> At length I became as rich as the Gurneys—
> An incubus then I thought her,
> So I threw over that rich attorney's
> Elderly, ugly daughter.
> The rich attorney my character high
> Tried vainly to disparage—
> And now, if you please, I'm ready to try
> This Breach of Promise of Marriage!

The judge's attitude towards the sanctity of marriage thus firmly established, the case proceeds. Legal precedent is nicely lampooned, moreover, when counsel for the plaintiff, referring to a law book, comes out with this remarkable statement:

> In the reign of James the Second
> It was generally reckoned
> As a rather serious crime
> To marry two wives at a time!

Eventually the judge, getting fed up with the proceedings and increasingly enamoured of the plaintiff anyway, provides the ideal solution:

> All the legal furies seize you
> No proposal seems to please you,
> I can't stay up here all day,
> I must shortly get away.
> Barristers and you attorneys
> Set out on your homeward journeys;
> Gentle, simple-minded Usher
> Get you, if you like, to Russia;
> Put your briefs upon the shelf,
> I will marry her *myself.*

A typically absurd Gilbertian finish!

W. S. Gilbert returned to the law in a big way in *Iolanthe* (first performed in 1882). The basic story-line is entirely idiotic: namely, the life and love of Strephon, son of a *fairy* mother (Iolanthe) and a *mortal* father (who turns out to be none other than the Lord Chancellor!) The Lord Chancellor is rightly regarded as one of Gilbert's most effective comic characters; he certainly made very good use of his legal knowledge in creating him; and, on stage, the part was first played by George Grossmith who was also the original John Wellington Wells in *The Sorcerer* (1877), Sir Joseph Porter in *H.M.S Pinafore* (1878), Major-General Stanley in the London production of *The Pirates of Penzance* (1880), Reginald Bunthorne in *Patience* (1881), King Gama in *Princess Ida* (1884), KoKo in *The Mikado* (1885), Robin Oakapple in *Ruddigore* (1887) and Jack Point in *The Yeomen of the Guard* (1888). Together with his brother Weedon Grossmith, moreover, he was to achieve virtual immortality in his own right as co-author of *The Diary of a Nobody* published in 1892.

In Act 1 of *Iolanthe* the Lord Chancellor tells the story of his progress from young barrister to his present exalted position at the apex of the legal profession. And, throughout, Gilbert is clearly at his sardonic best:

> When I went to the bar as a very young man
> (Said I to myself—said I)
> I'll work on a new and original plan,
> (Said I to myself—said I)
> I'll never assume that a rogue or a thief
> Is a gentleman worthy of implicit belief,
> Because his attorney has sent me a brief
> (Said I to myself—said I)
>
> Ere I go into court I will read my brief through,
> (Said I to myself—said I)
> And I'll never take work I'm unable to do,
> (Said I to myself—said I)
>
> My learned profession I'll never disgrace,
> By taking a fee with a grin on my face,
> When I haven't been there to attend to the case,
> (Said I to myself—said I)

I'll never throw dust in a juryman's eyes
(Said I to myself—said I)
Or hoodwink a judge who is not over-wise
(Said I to myself—said I)
Or assume that the witnesses summoned in force
In Exchequer, Queen's Bench, Common Pleas or Divorce,
Have perjured themselves as a matter of course
(Said I to myself—said I)

In other professions in which men engage,
(Said I to myself—said I)
The Army, the Navy, the Church, and the Stage,
(Said I to myself—said I)
Professional licence, if carried too far,
Your chance of promotion will certainly mar—
And I fancy the rule might apply to the Bar,
(Said I to myself—said I)

In another song from Act 1 of *Iolanthe* Gilbert's Lord Chancellor, in not dissimilar vein, satirises the practice of wardship:

The Law is the true embodiment
Of everything that's excellent.
It has no kind of fault or flaw,
And I, my Lords, embody the Law.
The constitutional guardian I
Of pretty young Wards in Chancery,
All very agreeable girls—and none
Are over the age of twenty-one.
A pleasant occupation for
A rather susceptible Chancellor!

But though the compliment implied
Inflates me with legitimate pride,
It nevertheless can't be denied

> That it has its inconvenient side.
> For I'm not so old, and not so plain,
> And I'm quite prepared to marry again,
> But there'd be the deuce to play in the Lords
> If I fell in love with one of my Wards!
> Which rather tries my temper, for
> I'm *such* a susceptible Chancellor!
>
> And every one who'd marry a Ward
> Must come to me for my accord,
> And in my court I sit all day,
> Giving agreeable girls away,
> With one for him—and one for he—
> And one for you—and one for ye—
> And one for thou—and one for thee—
> But never, oh, never a one for me!
> Which is exasperating for
> A highly susceptible Chancellor!

Almost three years earlier, in *The Pirates of Penzance*, Gilbert had very much enjoyed himself at the expense of the police. His nervous and neurotic policemen, with their lamentable lack of enthusiasm for meeting up with a horde of cut-throat pirates, have a universal appeal. Major-General Stanley's daughter Mabel exhorts them:

> Go, ye heroes, go to glory,
> Though you die in combat gory,
> Ye shall live in song and story.
> Go to immortality!
> Go to death, and go to slaughter;
> Die, and every Cornish daughter
> With her tears your grave shall water.
> Go, ye heroes, go and die!

The police, however, are very reluctant to do anything of the kind! 'These expressions are well meant' they sing, but they are *not*:

Calculated men to cheer …
Who are going to meet their fate
In a highly nervous state.

And, in Act 2, the Sergeant of Police *explains* their lack of enthusiasm for the job:

When a felon's not engaged in his employment—
Or maturing his felonious little plans—
His capacity for innocent enjoyment—
Is just as great as any honest man's—
Our feelings we with difficulty smother
When constabulary duty's to be done—
Ah, take one consideration with another—
A policeman's lot is not a happy one.

When the enterprising burglar's not a-burgling—
When the cut-throat isn't occupied in crime—
He loves to hear the little brook a-gurgling—
And listen to the merry village chime—
When the coster's finished jumping on his mother—
He loves to lie a-basking in the sun—
Ah, take one consideration with another—
A policeman's lot is not a happy one.

When this song is over the police, hearing the pirates are coming, cannot hide themselves fast enough!

2

Army, Navy and the Military Scene

If the law was badly in need of reform by the time William Gladstone put together his first Liberal ministry at the end of 1868, the Army was even more so. The Crimean War (1854-1856), which W. S. Gilbert was just too late to experience in person, had highlighted many defects but little was done to remedy them in the years that followed. Most of the soldiers came from the poorest and least educated sections of society: not surprisingly, therefore, their lives were grim indeed. The majority of the officers, by contrast, came from the upper classes and were essentially amateurs: a man bought a commission in the Army because it was 'the done thing' (like hunting in the country or 'the season' in town). And, as the Crimean War had demonstrated all too graphically, although such men may have had courage, they frequently lacked much in the way of military expertise.

In 1868 Gladstone appointed Edward Cardwell as his secretary of war and, at last, here was a man who not only recognised the urgent need for reform but was also prepared to take on the powerful opposition of vested interests (led by the duke of Cambridge, who was Commander-in-Chief, and most existing army officers, as well as the majority of peers and Conservative members of parliament). Before long he abolished flogging in the army in peacetime and introduced a much-needed system of short service: both reforms were vigorously opposed by senior officers. Most importantly, and best remembered, in 1871 Cardwell put together a bill seeking to abolish the practice of purchasing commissions in the army: again, this was strongly resisted by most officers and, indeed, by upper-class society in general (see page 73). Enjoying, as he did, the wholehearted support of Gladstone, he managed to get the bill through nevertheless. These, and other, reforms greatly improved the efficiency of the Army, opening up the possibility of a career in the service for men without wealth and family influence. Hence the much improved fighting record of British troops overseas in the last three decades of the nineteenth century. True, there were still plenty of officers of the 'old school' (among them the duke of Cambridge, sworn enemy to all progress, who somehow managed to remain commander-in-chief until 1895!) but there also emerged men like Sir Garnet Wolseley who were of a very different background and calibre (see page 79).

Clearly, there was plenty of promising material here not only for Gilbert's wit but also his fierce patriotism. In *Patience* (1881) the 35th Dragoon Guards sing on their very first appearance:

> The soldiers of our Queen
> Are linked in friendly tether;
> Upon the battle scene
> They fight the foe together.
> There every mother's son
> Prepared to fight and fall is;
> The enemy of one
> The enemy of all is.

In *Utopia Limited* (1893) Princess Zara brings over from England Captain Fitzbattleaxe (clearly an officer of the new type):

> When Britain sounds the trump of war
> (And Europe trembles)
> The army of the conqueror
> In serried ranks assembles;
> 'Tis then this warrior's eyes and sabre gleam
> For our protection—
> He represents a military scheme
> In all its proud perfection!

There is also the very *British* Japanese Army we find in *The Mikado* (1885):

> Our warriors in serried ranks
> Never quail—or conceal it if they do.
> And I shouldn't be surprised if nations trembled
> Before the mighty troops of Titipu.

Major-General Stanley in *The Pirates of Penzance* (1879) and the duke of Plaza-Toro in *The Gondoliers* (1889) are military gentleman of *very* different types: it seems more than likely, moreover, that Gilbert's model for Stanley was Sir Garnet Wolseley, while that for the duke of Plaza-Toro may will have been the reactionary duke of Cambridge. The swashbuckling Wolseley was clearly very much a Victorian military whiz-kid and thoroughly disliked as such by the establishment. Indeed, he once wrote:

> All other pleasures pale before the intense, the maddening, delight of leading man into the midst of an enemy or to the assault of some well-defended place.

Wolseley fought in the Burma War of 1852, the Crimean War of 1854-1856, the Indian Mutiny of 1857, the American Civil War of 1861-1865, the Canadian rebellion of 1869 and the Ashanti War of 1873. Then, in 1879, he was sent to South Africa to replace Lord Chelmsford who had bungled things badly there. Queen Victoria was *not* pleased: she not only objected to the treatment of Chelmsford but also expressed strong disapproval of Wolseley who, as a liberal-minded supporter of Cardwell's reforms, was anathema to her cousin the duke of Cambridge. Conservative party leader Benjamin Disraeli (Prime Minister 1874-1880) wrote to Lady Chesterfield: 'The Horse Guards are furious, the Princes all raging, and every mediocrity as jealous as if he had prevented him from conquering the world'. To Queen Victoria *herself* he wrote: 'It is quite true that Wolseley is an egotist and a braggart. So was Nelson'. A few years later, in 1885, it was Wolseley who was despatched to relieve Khartoum and, eventually, he replaced the duke of Cambridge as commander-in-chief in 1895.

W. S. Gilbert only rarely referred to living Englishmen *by name* in the operas: Sir Garnet Wolseley is an exception. In the catalogue of 'all the remarkable people in history' rattled off by Colonel Calverley in *Patience*, the 'skill of Sir Garnet in thrashing a cannibal' is cited alongside the 'genius of Bismarck devising a plan' and the 'narrative powers of Dickens and Thackeray'. Moreover, Major-General Stanley in *The Pirates of Penzance* (an opera first performed at the end of 1879, the year Wolseley went to South Africa) certainly has *many* of the characteristics of Sir Garnet: indeed, when George Grossmith played Stanley in the London production, he was even made up to look like Wolseley! Both Stanley and Wolseley held the same rank. Stanley was an orphan while Wolseley lost his father when he was only seven. Gilbert may well have been satirising Wolseley's desire to escape from his humble origins when he has Stanley tell Frederic that he has bought an estate (together with a chapel and the ancestors buried in it): 'I don't know whose ancestors they *were*', he remarks, 'but I know whose ancestors they are *now*'. Above all, both Stanley and Wolseley had very high opinions of themselves. Wolseley himself, moreover, was more than happy to be taken as 'the very model of a modern major general'; he enjoyed singing Stanley's famous patter-song to his friends and family; and, seemingly, he revelled in the reflected glory that *The Pirates of Penzance* brought him. Perhaps he should have studied the lyrics more carefully! It was hardly complimentary, for instance, to be taken as the inspiration for an army officer who knows about almost everything *except* military matters and a general who possesses no more grasp of tactics them 'a novice in the nunnery':

I am the very model of a modern Major-General,
I've information vegetable, animal, and mineral,
I know the kings of England, and I quote the fights historical
From Marathon to Waterloo, in order categorical;
I'm very well acquainted, too, with matters mathematical,
I understand equations, both the simple and quadratical,
About binomial theorem I'm teeming with a lot o' news,
With many cheerful facts about the square of the hypotenuse.

I'm very good at integral and differential calculus;
I know the scientific names of beings animalculous:
In short, in matters vegetable, animal, and mineral,
I am the very model of a modern Major-General.

I know our mythic history, King Arthur's and Sir Caradoc's;
I answer hard acrostics, I've a pretty taste for paradox,
I quote in elegiacs all the crimes of Heliogabalus,
In conics I can floor peculiarities parabolous;
I can tell undoubted Raphaels from Gerard Dows and Zoffanies,
I know the croaking chorus from the Frogs of Aristophanes!
Then I can hum a fugue of which I've heard the music's din afore,
And whistle all the airs from that infernal nonsense Pinafore.

Then I can write a washing bill in Babylonic cuneiform,
And tell you ev'ry detail of Caractacus's uniform:
In short, in matters vegetable, animal, and mineral,
I am the very model of a modern Major-General.

In fact, when I know what is meant by 'mamelon' and 'ravelin',
When I can tell at sight a Mauser rifle from a javelin,
When such affairs as sorties and surprises I'm more wary at,
And when I know precisely what is meant by 'commissariat',
When I have learnt what progress has been made in modern gunnery,
When I know more of tactics than a novice in a nunnery—
In short, when I've a smattering of elemental strategy—
You'll say a better Major-General has never sat a-gee.

For my military knowledge, though I'm plucky and adventury,
Has only been brought down to the beginning of the century;
But still, in matters vegetable, animal, and mineral,
I am the very model of a modern Major-General.

If Edward Cardwell's military reforms were by no means as thorough in practice as they were in theory, much of the blame can be heaped on the duke of Cambridge. The best regiments, at least, continued to be officered by the upper classes and, even in the 1890s, the lower ranks were still too often drawn from the dregs of society. Gilbert clearly had the *old style* army officer in mind (perhaps, indeed, Cambridge himself) when reviewing the duke of Plaza-Toro's undistinguished military career in *The Gondoliers* (first performed in December 1889):

In enterprise of martial kind,
    When there was any fighting,
He led his regiment from behind—
He found it less exciting.
But when away his regiment ran,
His place was at the fore, O—
That celebrated, cultivated, underrated
    nobleman, the Duke of Plaza-Toro!

When, to evade Destruction's hand,
To hide they all proceeded,
No soldier in that gallant band
Hid half as well as he did.
He lay concealed throughout the war,
And so preserved his gore, O!
That unaffected, undetected, well-connected
              warrior, the Duke of Plaza-Toro!

When told that they would all be shot
Unless they left the service,
That hero hesitated not,
So marvellous his nerve is.
He sent his resignation in,
The first of all his corps, O!
That very knowing, overflowing, easy-going
              Paladin, the Duke of Plaza-Toro!

*   *   *   *   *

Later Victorian patriotic Englishmen, of whom W. S. Gilbert was a prime example, had an especial pride in the Navy: indeed, the Navy had no small opinion of itself! Yet the social structure of the Navy, while less archaic than the Army, nevertheless also owed a great deal to privilege. Even as late as 1897 the officers of the executive arm included two princes, two dukes, an earl, two viscounts, four barons, eight baronets, and thirty-five honourables, while there were no fewer than twelve titled captains! Inevitably, perhaps, men like these were too much inclined to live in the past, to regret the passing of the great days of sail, and to regard engines (and those who had the misfortune to look after them) with considerable distaste. Hardly surprisingly, too, the Navy itself was becoming increasingly out-of-date in the later nineteenth century, not least where armaments were concerned: even those guns ships did have, we are told, tended to be fired as seldom as possible so as not to damage the paintwork! W. S. Gilbert himself, while fully prepared to lampoon the navy in *H.M.S. Pinafore*, nevertheless had much affection for it; he knew a great deal about ships and sailors as well, not least because his father had been a naval surgeon; and when he decided to set a comic opera on board one of Her Majesty's vessels, he was determined to be accurate at all costs: indeed, he paid several visits to Portsmouth and carefully studied the deck of HMS *Victory*. The critic of *The Standard* had this to say of the result:

> So perfect a quarterdeck as that of H.M.S. *Pinafore* has assuredly *never* been put on the stage. Every block and rope to the minutest detail is in its place. In fact, it is an exact model of what it represents.

Gilbert himself wrote to Sullivan when working on the opera:

> The uniforms of the officers and crew will be effective. The chorus will look like sailors and I will ask to have their uniforms made for them at Portsmouth.

As for Captain Corcoran of H.M.S. *Pinafore*, he is a splendid example of what so many later Victorian naval captains were actually like: a strict disciplinarian who nevertheless admits to commanding 'a right good crew', he is proud to be 'related to a peer' and cannot contemplate the idea of his daughter marrying a common sailor. He is certainly very patriotic as well. Indeed, when he reappears in *Utopia Limited*, he introduces himself thus:

> I'm Captain Corcoran, KCB,
> I'll teach you how we rule the sea,
> And terrify the simple Gauls;
> And how the Saxon and the Celt
> Their Europe-shaking blows have dealt …

What probably did most to ensure the success of *H.M.S. Pinafore* was that audiences could only too easily recognise the great similarity between Gilbert's Sir Joseph Porter, first lord of the Admiralty, and Disraeli's recent appointment of W. H. Smith to that exalted office in reality! Gilbert himself wrote to Sullivan, some months before the opera was first staged, suggesting:

> … a song for the First Lord tracing his career as an office boy in a cotton-broker's office, traveller, junior partner and First Lord of Britain's Navy. I think a splendid

song could be made of this. Of course there will be no *personality* in this—the fact the First Lord in the opera is a radical of the most pronounced type will do away with *any* suspicion that W. H. Smith is intended.

Nevertheless, despite a character make-up designed to confuse the issue, late Victorian audiences were in no doubt whatever as to whom Porter was meant to be in caricature. W. H. Smith's father had made himself the leading newsagent in the country; Smith himself ensured the future prosperity of the business by securing the exclusive rights to sell newspapers and books on all the important railway stations of England. Returned to Parliament for the first time in 1868, he obtained a junior Treasury post in Disraeli's Conservative ministry in 1874. Following the death of George Ward Hunt in 1877 (see page 76), Disraeli decided to appoint him First Lord of the Admiralty (the year before *H.M.S. Pinafore* hit the stage).

Traditionally, the office of first lord of the Admiralty had been monopolised by men of high social status: W. H. Smith, by contrast, was regarded by many as a London tradesman pure and simple. Disraeli himself was only too well aware of what might prove a tricky appointment: indeed, he wrote to Queen Victoria warning that Smith was 'purely a man of the middle class'. The Queen was *not* enthusiastic, replying that she was:

> … prepared to agree if necessary, but she *fears* it may *not please* the Navy, in which service so many of the *highest rank* serve and who claim to be of equal rank with the Army, if a man of the Middle Class is placed above them in that very high post.

When Smith was duly appointed, she remarked that he must not:

> … lord it over the Navy (which almost every First Lord does) and be a little modest and not *act* the Lord High Admiral which would be offensive to the service.

To make matters even worse, Smith was not only middle class but also a man of staunch Methodist principles: hence, no doubt, Sir Joseph Porter's horror in *H.M.S. Pinafore* when confronted by bad language on board ship! And, perhaps, it is also worth noticing the similarities between Smith's early career and that of W. S. Gilbert himself. Here, meanwhile, is Sir Joseph Porter's version of *his* Smith-like rise to become the 'monarch of the sea' and 'ruler of the Queen's Navee':

When I was a lad I served a term
As office boy to an Attorney's firm.
I cleaned the windows and I swept the floor,
And I polished up the handle of the big front door.
I polished up that handle so carefullee
That now I am the Ruler of the Queen's Navee!

As office boy I made such a mark
That they gave me the post of a junior clerk.
I served the writs with a smile so bland,
And I copied all the letters in a big round hand—
I copied all the letters in a hand so free,
That now I am the Ruler of the Queen's Navee!

In serving writs I made such a name
That an articled clerk I soon became;
I wore clean collars and a brand new suit
For the pass examination at the Institute.
That pass examination did so well for me,
That now I am the Ruler of the Queen's Navee!

Of legal knowledge I acquired such a grip
That they took me into the partnership.
And that junior partnership, I ween,
Was the only ship that I ever had seen.
But that kind of ship so suited me,
That now I am the Ruler of the Queen's Navee!

I grew so rich that I was sent
By a pocket borough into Parliament.
I always voted at my party's call,
And I never thought of thinking for myself at all.
I thought so little, they rewarded me
By making me the Ruler of the Queen's Navee!

Now, landsmen all, wherever you may be,
If you want to rise to the top of the tree,
If your soul isn't fettered to an office stool,
Be careful to be guided by this golden rule—
Stick close to your desks and never go to sea,
And you all may be Rulers of the Queen's Navee!

Disraeli himself seems to have been tickled pink by the send-up of Smith: in a letter written soon after the first production of *H.M.S. Pinafore*, he even referred to him as 'Pinafore Smith'! Smith, predictably, found it all less than funny. There is a nice story of a visit made by him to launch a ship at Devonport. To avoid embarrassment, a message was sent to the bandmaster of the Royal Marines Band ordering him *not* to include any music from *H.M.S. Pinafore*. Unfortunately, due to a bureaucratic bungle of the sort calculated to gladden Gilbert's heart, the message was *reversed* and, as a result, the hapless Smith was actually *greeted* by the strains of 'When I was a lad'. As if that was not enough, the so-called Tory Democrat Lord Randolph Churchill could not resist labelling Smith (and another middle-class man Richard Cross) as not only 'bourgeois placemen' but also the veritable 'Marshall and Snelgrove' of the Conservative party. Again, a remark in distinctly Gilbertian mode!

3

Politics and the Political Scene

Inevitably, in the Savoy Operas, W. S. Gilbert has much to say about Victorian politics and the political scene. Even monarchy figures occasionally. Guiseppe Palmieri, in *The Gondoliers*, is a convinced republican (reflecting a powerful minority viewpoint in later Victorian England), at any rate until he discovers he might be heir to the kingdom of Barataria. At once his republicanism shows signs of crumbling:

> Well, of course, there are kings and kings. When I say I detest *bad* kings, I can nevertheless conceive a kind of king—an ideal king—who will be absolutely unobjectionable. A king, for instance, who would abolish taxes and make everything cheap.

Gilbert and Sullivan certainly had royal fans of their own. Several members of the royal family attended the first night of *The Mikado* in 1885 and Queen Victoria herself sent for the music. In March 1891 a special performance of *The Gondoliers* was mounted at Windsor Castle (the first theatrical performance seen there since Prince Albert's death in 1861). The queen herself attended and was, by all accounts, delighted with what she saw. W. S. Gilbert was less happy when he discovered his name had been missed off the programme! Benjamin Disraeli and William Gladstone, too, are on record as enjoying the operas. Disraeli, it seems, particularly delighted in *H.M.S. Pinafore* and its wicked caricature of W. H. Smith. Gladstone, apparently, was no less pleased by *Iolanthe*. At Sullivan's invitation he saw the opera within a week of its first performance and, on 6 December 1882, wrote to him from 10 Downing Street:

> … I must thankfully acknowledge the great pleasure which the entertainment gave me. Nothing, I thought, could be happier than the manner in which the comic strain of the piece was blended with its harmonies of sight and sound, so good in taste and so admirable in execution from beginning to end.

Six months later Sullivan was knighted!

Foreign reactions to the operas were not always so good. For instance there were complaints that references in *Ruddigore* (1887) constituted an insult to French national pride: indeed, there was even an attempt to get the opera taken off. Yet, as a contemporary critic remarked:

> It is well to remember that Messrs Gilbert and Sullivan have long tried—in vain!—to foist one of their operettas on Paris: this *may* be their *revenge* out of spite.

More absurd still was the reaction at home to a projected revival of *The Mikado* in 1907. Britain had concluded an alliance with *Japan* in 1902: consequently, on the eve of an official visit to these shores by Prince Fushimi in 1907, the Lord Chamberlain forbad *all* stage presentations of *The Mikado* out of deference to our new Japanese allies (see page 95). There was a considerable outcry, not least in the House of Commons: one irate MP even asked Prime Minister Campbell-Bannerman whether he would instruct the Lord Chamberlain to prohibit productions of *Hamlet* on the grounds that it portrayed a king of Denmark as a murderer and might therefore cause offence to another friendly power! W. S. Gilbert himself was furious, no doubt remembering his own strictures on censorship and the Lord Chamberlain in *Utopia Limited* (1893), where Phantis remarks:

> Are you aware that the Lord Chamberlain, who has his own views as to the best means of elevating the national drama, has declined to license *any* play that is not in blank verse and three hundred years old!

G. K. Chesterton certainly pinpointed the absurdity of the ban nicely when he declared that, in *The Mikado*, Gilbert:

> … pursued and persecuted the evils of *modern England* till they had literally not a leg to stand on; exactly as Swift did under the allegory of *Gulliver's Travels*. Yet it is the solid and comic fact that *The Mikado* was actually *forbidden* because it was a satire on Japan … I doubt if there is a single joke in the whole play that fits the Japanese. But *all* the jokes in the play fit the *English*…

Early in 1908 the Lord Chamberlain relented!

W. S. Gilbert, in general, was nothing if not *patriotic*. Even in *The Mikado* there is reference to 'the idiot who praises with enthusiastic tones all centuries but this and every country but his own'; in *H.M.S. Pinafore* we find the archetypal patriot who, 'in spite of all temptations to belong to other nations, remains an Englishman'; and in *The Pirates of Penzance*, when called upon to 'yield in Queen Victoria's name', the pirates do so '*at once*, with humbled mien, because, with all our faults, we love our queen'. Gilbert could certainly be very cutting, however, when it came to *political parties* and *party politics*. In *Utopia Limited*, perhaps the most biting of all the Savoy Operas despite its indifferent reception at the time (1893) and virtual neglect ever since, the absurdities of the party system provide a central theme. English institutions are so successfully transplanted into the south Pacific island of Utopia, indeed, that life there becomes intolerably *boring*: the Army and the Navy are so successfully remodelled that neighbouring nations disarm; such drastic sanitary laws are introduced that the island's doctors are reduced to starvation; and a new legal system results in the extinction of both litigation and crime! Then suddenly, at the end of the opera, Princess Zara remembers that she has forgotten to introduce the most essential element of English life: political parties. It hits her like a bolt from the blue:

> Government by Party! Introduce *that* great and glorious element—at once the bulwark and foundation of England's greatness—and all will be well! No political measures will endure, because one Party will assuredly undo all that the other Party has done; inexperienced civilians will govern your Army and your Navy; no social reforms will be attempted, because out of vice, squalor, and drunkenness no political capital is to be made; and while grouse is to be shot, and foxes worried to death, the legislative action of the country will be at a standstill. Then there will be sickness in plenty, endless lawsuits, crowded jails, interminable confusion in the Army and the Navy, and, in short, general and unexampled prosperity!

Then, of course, there is *Iolanthe*! Over four decades back Kenneth Baker, then a rising Conservative politician, suggested that the chief characters in that opera are, in fact, deliberate representations of leading Victorian politicians: the Lord Chancellor, for instance, was based on William Gladstone, Strephon on Lord Randolph Churchill, Lord Mountararat on Lord Hartington, the Fairy Queen on Queen Victoria and Private Willis on none other than the queen's Scottish gillie John Brown. A compelling thesis if not, perhaps, an entirely convincing one! Nevertheless, it is in *Iolanthe* that we find Gilbert's most evocative send-up of the party system, splendidly voiced by Private Willis at the beginning of Act 2 of the opera:

> When all night long a chap remains
> On sentry-go, to chase monotony
> He exercises of his brains,
> That is, assuming that he's got any.
> Though never nurtured in the lap
> Of luxury, yet I admonish you,
> I am an intellectual chap,
> And think of things that would astonish you.
> I often think it's comical—Fal, lal, la!
> How Nature always does contrive—Fal, lal, la!
> That every boy and every gal
> That's born into the world alive
> Is either a little Liberal
> Or else a little Conservative! Fal, lal, la!
>
> When in that House MP's divide,
> If they've a brain and cerebellum, too,
> They've got to leave that brain outside,
> And vote just as their leaders tell 'em to.
> But then the prospect of a lot
> Of dull MP's in close proximity,
> All thinking for themselves, is what
> No man can face with equanimity.
> Then let's rejoice with loud Fal la—Fal lal la!
> That Nature always does contrive—Fal lal la!
> That every boy and every gal
> That's born into this world alive
> Is either a little Liberal
> Or else a little Conservative! Fal lal la!

4

Society and the Social Scene

Most English people, if they ponder Victorian times at all, probably picture a society in which the upper and middle classes led an enviably comfortable life, with plenty of servants and an abundance of material wealth, while the masses struggled along in a manner guaranteed to send shudders down the spine of any self-respecting socialist. Yet, in its heyday at least, here was a society that professed to be upright, hard-working, clean-living and, above all, God-fearing; Evangelicalism, with its stress on prayer, preaching and Bible-reading, sought to provide a strong moral cement; and self-improvement was judged to be in every way admirable, hedonism entirely to be frowned upon. W. S. Gilbert himself grew up in, and was fashioned by, this society; however, by the time he came to pen the Savoy Operas, traditional Victorian values and principles were clearly beginning to be questioned and undermined. Evangelicalism's foundations came under attack from growing Anglo-Catholicism on the one hand and rationalism on the other; Bible-reading and church-going began to decline as more and more alternatives became available; and, eventually, the revival of hedonism came to threaten even notions of sobriety, hard work and self-improvement. The growing popularity of Gilbert and Sullivan comic operas from the later 1870s, moreover, is an all too clear reflection of society's increasing desire for, and delight in, light entertainment.

W. S. Gilbert has relatively little to say about religion in his librettos (perhaps because, in this sensitive area at least, he was anxious not to give offence) but he certainly did not ignore it entirely. The kng of Barataria in *The Gondoliers*, for instance, is a 'misguided monarch' who 'abandoned the creed of his forefathers and became a Wesleyan Methodist of the most bigoted and persecuting type' while, had Gilbert stuck to an early plan for *Patience*, it might well have involved a great deal of satirical comment on both lesser dignitaries in the Anglican church and their admirers. A group of dashing young cavalry officers, in pursuit of a coterie of desirable young ladies, would have found themselves cut out by a couple of curates; eventually, in order to win back the maidens' favour, Gilbert then envisaged them surrendering their commissions and becoming clergymen themselves! At a late stage in the opera's preparation, however, he had second thoughts about the comic clerics and decided, instead, to caricature the contemporary aesthetic movement. 'Although it is almost two thirds finished', he wrote to Sullivan at the beginning of November 1880, 'I don't feel comfortable' about the piece:

> I mistrust the clerical element. I feel hampered by the restrictions which the nature of the subject places upon my freedom of action, and I want to revert to my old idea of rivalry between two aesthetic fanatics, worshipped by a chorus of female devotees. I can get much more fun out of the subject, as I propose to alter it, and the general scheme of the piece will remain as at present. The Hussars will all become aesthetic young men (abandoning their profession for the purpose). In this latter capacity they will all carry lilies in their hands, wear long hair, and stand in stained-glass attitudes.

The Victorian aesthetic movement, pioneered by a group of super-aesthetes who contemptuously rejected the previous generation's art as disastrously infected by morality and proclaimed instead the doctrine of 'Art for Art's sake', was at its height in 1880. Most famously, Oscar Wilde, even while still at Oxford University in the later 1870s, developed a reputation as an exponent of 'Art for Art's sake'; his rooms in Magdalen College became notorious for their exotic splendour; and, by the time he left Oxford in 1879, he had already become sufficiently well-known to be caricatured in the satirical magazine *Punch*. By then, too, he had become utterly identified with the aesthetic cult and its symbols: long hair, velvet jackets, peacocks' feathers, sunflowers, carnations and, of course, lilies.

W. S. Gilbert, there can be no doubt, found the 'modern school of lily-bearing poets' (as he called it) completely preposterous and, as a result, sent it up with a vengeance in *Patience* (for which, incidentally, he also put together his most accomplished and sophisticated libretto). Oscar Wilde himself seems to have attended the first night (on 23 April 1881) and the critic of the *Sporting Times*, for one, could hardly contain his emotions:

Pending the arrival of Dr Sullivan in the conductor's chair, I gazed with furtive curiosity on my neighbours, and confess that so many representatives of the Good, the Beautiful and the True filled me with surpassing awe.… A fierce clamour of screams, yells and hisses which descended from the gallery signalled the arrival of Mr Oscar Wilde himself.… There, with the sacred daffodil, stood the exponent of uncut hair, Ajax-like defying the Gods.

Patience clearly appealed to late Victorian audiences although, unlike most Gilbert and Sullivan operas, it can puzzle *modern* ones. Richard D'Oyly Carte, indeed, believed it would perplex *contemporary Americans* too and, for that reason, it may well have been he who despatched Oscar Wilde on a lecture tour across the Atlantic in 1882 to prepare them for it! As a result, according to Max Beerbohm (who actually saw Wilde while he was there touring the States), the aesthete became a veritable 'sandwich board for *Patience*' (see page 85). The opera itself highlights two aesthetic young men in particular (Reginald Bunthorne, the original, and Archibald Grosvenor, the look-alike) and both were clearly inspired by Oscar Wilde himself. Yet Bunthorne openly admits, in what is perhaps the best of all Gilbert's patter-songs, that, in fact, he is no more than an aesthetic sham:

Am I alone, And unobserved? I am!

Then let me own I'm an æsthetic sham!

This air severe Is but a mere Veneer!

This cynic smile Is but a wile Of guile!

This costume chaste Is but good taste Misplaced!

Let me confess!

A languid love for lilies does not blight me!

Lank limbs and haggard cheeks do *not* delight me!

I do *not* care for dirty greens By any means.

I do *not* long for all one sees That's Japanese.

    I am not fond of uttering platitudes In stained-glass attitudes.

In short, my mediævalism's affectation,

Born of a morbid love of admiration!

If you're anxious for to shine in the high

                æsthetic line as a man of culture rare,

You must get up all the germs of the transcendental

terms, and plant them ev'rywhere.
You must lie upon the daisies and discourse in
novel phrases of your complicated
state of mind,
The meaning doesn't matter if it's only idle
chatter of a transcendental kind.
And ev'ry one will say, As you walk your mystic way,
'If this young man expresses himself in
terms too deep for *me*,
Why, what a very singularly deep young man
this deep young man must be!'

Be eloquent in praise of the very dull old days
which have long since passed away,
And convince 'em, if you can, that the reign
of good Queen Anne was Culture's
palmiest day.
Of course you will pooh-pooh whatever's
fresh and new, and declare it's
crude and mean,
For Art stopped short in the cultivated court
of the Empress Josephine.
And ev'ryone will say, As you walk your
mystic way,
'If that's not good enough for him which is
good enough for *me*,
Why, what a very cultivated kind of youth
this kind of youth must be!'

Then a sentimental passion of a vegetable
fashion must excite your languid
spleen,
An attachment *à la Plato* for a bashful
young potato, or a not-too-French
French bean!

Though the Philistines may jostle, you will

rank as an apostle in the high æsthetic band,

If you walk down Piccadilly with a poppy

or a lily in your mediæval hand.

And ev'ryone will say, As you walk your

flow'ry way,

'If he's content with a vegetable love

which would certainly not suit *me,*

Why, what a most particularly pure young man

this pure young man must be!'

Incidentally, Bunthorne's protestation that he does not 'long for all one sees that's Japanese' is clearly a reference to the Japanese craze of the 1870s and 1880s, culminating in the Japanese exhibition at Knightsbridge in 1885. And Gilbert clearly had Japanese mania even more in mind when writing *The Mikado* (which had its first performance on 14 March 1885).

Education was another prime target for W. S. Gilbert's wit, most notably competitive examinations and the education of women. By an Order in Council of 1870, the Liberal Prime Minister William Gladstone made entry to most branches of the Civil Service (except the Foreign Office) open to competition: henceforth any educated and able young man could embark on a career in the public service, providing he managed to pass a competitive examination. Consequently, it need come as no surprise to find Sir Joseph Porter, in *H.M.S. Pinafore*, anxious to stress *his* examination success as a factor in his rise to high office; as for Strephon, in *Iolanthe*, he even introduces a bill into parliament designed to throw the peerage open to competitive examination. The development of women's education, particularly the foundation of Girton College, Cambridge, in 1873, provided a major theme for *Princess Ida* (first performed in January 1884). Here we find King Gama's daughter, Princess Ida, has established in Castle Adamant a university of 100 females; present, too, is Lady Psyche, Professor of Humanities, who advocates the reading of classics like Ovid and Aristophenes (suitably bowdlerised, of course); and, as an additional bonus, there is Lady Blanche, Professor of Abstract Science, a highly ambitious and formidable female don. Gilbert's *own* attitude towards it all is firmly expressed by Florian:

> A woman's college! maddest folly going!
> What can girls learn within its walls worth knowing?
> I'll lay a crown (the Princess shall decide it)
> I'll teach them twice as much in half-an-hour outside it.

Gilbert addressed the same subject once more in *Utopia Limited*, where Princess Zara returns to her father's court (after five years in England) with a degree from Girton and a passion for all things Anglo-Saxon. In *Ruddigore* he had a go at late Victorian melodrama; while in *Princess Ida* he clearly had Darwinism, as well as female education, firmly in his sights:

> A Lady fair, of lineage high,
> Was loved by an Ape, in the days gone by.
> The Maid was radiant as the sun,
> The Ape was a most unsightly one …
> With a view to rise in the social scale,
> He shaved his bristles and he docked his tail …
> He bought white ties, and he bought dress suits,
> He crammed his feet into bright tight boots —
> And to start in life on a brand-new plan,
> He christened himself Darwinian Man!

And the song concludes :

> … Man, however well-behaved,
> At best is only a monkey shaved!

Limited liability companies, increasingly common in later Victorian England, did not meet with Gilbert's approval either. In *The Gondoliers* the penniless Duke of Plaza-Toro turns *himself* into a limited company, while in *Utopia Limited* it is said of the company promoter Mr Goldsbury:

> To speculators he supplies a grand financial leaven,
> Time was when *two* were company—but now it must be *seven*.

In fact, according to Goldsbury:

> … nothing that is planned by mortal head
> Is certain in this Vale of Sorrows—saving
> That one's Liability is Limited.

Indeed, he declared, Britain is now well on the way to being *governed* on joint stock principles! Finally, when King Paramount decides to register his *crown* under the 'Joint Stock Companies Act of Sixty-Two', Goldsbury goes one better and turns every man, woman and child in Utopia into a limited liability company. Income tax, too, comes in for comment in the Savoy operas. King Gama, in *Princess Ida*, gives as one of the reasons for his unpopularity:

> I know everybody's income and what everybody earns,
> and I carefully compare it with the Income Tax Returns.

That was in 1884. By the time *Ruddigore* was staged in 1887, however, the standard rate of income tax had risen from 5 pence to 7 pence in the pound, and when Sir Ruthven Murgatroyd tells the ghosts of his ancestors that he has made a false income tax return, they coolly reply:

> That's nothing. Nothing at all.
> Everybody does *that*. It's expected of you!

Clearly, W. S. Gilbert had a positive fixation when it came to social class and rank. In *The Sorcerer* (1877), for instance, Alexis is anxious to break down artificial barriers of rank, particularly as far as marriage is concerned:

Alexis

… I have made some converts to the principle, that men and women should be coupled in matrimony without distinction of rank. I have lectured on the subject at Mechanics' Institutes, and the mechanics were unanimous in favour of my views. I have preached in workhouses, beershops, and Lunatic Asylums, and I have been received with enthusiasm. I have addressed navvies on the advantages that would accrue to them if they married wealthy ladies of rank, and not a navvy dissented!

Aline

Noble fellows! And yet there are those who hold that the uneducated classes are not open to argument! And what do the countesses say?

Alexis

Why, at present, it can't be denied, the aristocracy stand aloof.

Aline

Ah, the working man is the true Intelligence after all!

Alexis

He *is* a noble creature when he is quite *sober.…*

Captain Corcoran in *H.M.S. Pinafore*, while declaring that he attaches little value to rank or wealth, nevertheless warns his daughter that 'the line must be drawn somewhere' and that her marriage to a humble tar would *not* make for happiness. This certainly contrasts with Sir Joseph Porter's firm statement in favour of *equality* in marriage and the irrelevance of social status. Ralph Rackstraw, the humble tar in question, is eloquent indeed:

> A suitor, lowly born,
> With hopeless passion torn,
> And poor beyond denying,
> Has dared for her to pine …
> Oh, pity, pity me—
> Our captain's daughter *she*,
> And I that lowly suitor!

W. S. Gilbert himself, there is no doubt, had a great respect for rank and title. Thus in *The Gondoliers*, when writing of a king who has abolished social distinctions, he declares:

> Lord Chancellors were cheap as sprats,
> And Bishops in their shovel hats
> Were plentiful as tabby cats …

> Prime Ministers and such as they
> Grew like asparagus in May,
> And Dukes were three a penny …
> With Admirals the oceans teemed …
> And Party Leaders you might meet
> In twos and threes in every street …

The song, predictably, concludes:

> When everyone is somebodee
> Then no one's anybody.

Gilbert certainly has a good deal to say *on behalf* of the aristocracy and the House of Lords. The pirates in *The Pirates of Penzance*, improbably enough, turn out to be noble born. As Ruth declares triumphantly:

> *They* are no members of the common throng;
> They are all *noblemen*, who have gone wrong!

To which Major-General Stanley responds:

> No Englishman unmoved that statement hears,
> Because, with all our faults, we love our House of Peers.

Lord Tolloller in *Iolanthe*, pleads on behalf of his fellow aristocrats:

> Spurn not the nobly born …
> Nor treat with virtuous scorn
> The well-connected.
> High rank involves no shame …
> Hearts just as pure and fair
> May beat in Belgrave Square
> As in the lowly air
> Of Seven Dials!

The lord's themselves have no doubts as to their own worth:

> We are peers of highest station,
> Paragons of legislation,
> Pillars of the British nation!

Nor has Lord Mountararat:

It so happens that if there is an institution in Great Britain which is *not* susceptible of any improvement *at all*, it is the House of Peers!

And, for Mountararat, peers and *patriotism* were virtually indivisible as well:

> When Britain really ruled the waves—
> (In good Queen Bess's time)
> The House of Peers made no pretence
> To intellectual eminence,
> Or scholarship sublime;
> Yet Britain won her proudest bays
> In good Queen Bess's glorious days!
>
> When Wellington thrashed Bonaparte,
> As every child can tell,
> The House of Peers, throughout the war,
> Did nothing in particular,
> And did it very well;
> Yet Britain set the world ablaze
> In good King George's glorious days!
>
> And while the House of Peers withholds
> Its legislative hand,
> And noble statesmen do not itch
> To interfere with matters which
> They do not understand,
> As bright will shine Great Britain's rays
> As in King George's glorious days!

Epilogue

Arthur Sullivan's compelling musical scores undoubtedly helped ensure the popularity and success of Savoy operas both in Victorian times and ever since; W. S. Gilbert's plots and lyrics were even more vitally important; and these, in turn, very much reflected the character and behaviour of Gilbert himself. It has been said of him, in particular, that he possessed all the prejudices of the Victorian professional class: he distrusted enthusiasm; he disliked the public display of emotion; he suspected all 'movements'; and he found most reformers extremely irritating. At heart, too, he was clearly a diehard Tory, but one who had little respect for men in high positions; he was a man who, while fiercely English, could nevertheless laugh at the jingoism of his times; and he was a comfortably middle-class Victorian who knew little of the life of the poor, cared less, and had no sympathy whatsoever for the early stirrings of socialism.

All this, clearly, very much underpins the topsy-turvy perspective on the world so evident in the Savoy operas; an imaginary world where characters frequently possess the opposite qualities to those they would probably display in reality; and an exaggerated caricature world such as might well be observed through the wrong end of a pair of opera glasses! The origins of topsy-turvydom *à la* W. S. Gilbert can be found in an 1870 Bab ballad 'My Dream' (where virtue is vice, soldiers are shot for being courageous and judges practise crime) and an 1874 stage extravaganza *Topsy-Turvydom* (where people are born old and gradually become younger, folly is honoured and wisdom despised, detestation is a compliment, and the national anthem is virtually a hymn of hate). By the time *The Pirates of Penzance* was staged in London in 1880, a contemporary commentator felt justified in concluding that, 'in a comical way', Gilbert:

… shows us all that is mean, and cruel, even in the world's heroes, and makes us laugh at them because we are convinced such faults are lingering in the breasts of the best of us.

And, as for the Japan of *The Mikado* (1885), it is surely none other than a distorted mirror-image reflection of Victorian England!

Obviously, historians must always exercise caution when drawing conclusions. Although Gilbert lampooned the House of Lords in *Iolanthe* (1882), for instance, he nevertheless loved it. When Liberals campaigning to reduce the powers of the Upper House in 1909 sought permission to quote from the opera, indeed, he responded robustly:

I cannot permit verses from *Iolanthe* to be used for electioneering purposes. They do *not* express my own views. They are supposed to be the views of the wrong-headed donkey who sings them.

Yet Gilbert's *own* peculiarly distorted and idiosyncratic portrayal of the world is surely never more apparent than in *Iolanthe*, not least at the end when all the peers sprout wings and depart for Fairyland:

> Soon as we may, Off and away!
> We'll commence our journey airy—
> Happy are we—As you can see,
> Every one is now a fairy!
>
> Though as a general rule we know
> Two strings go to every bow,
> Make up your minds that grief 'twill bring
> If you've two beaux to every string.
>
> Up in the sky, Ever so high,
> Pleasures come in endless series;
> We will arrange Happy exchange—
> House of Peers for House of Peris!

W. S. Gilbert at his most absurd and, courtesy of Arthur Sullivan's music, his most irresistible as well!

Select Bibliography

AYRE, L.,   *The Gilbert and Sullivan Companion* (1972)

BAILY, L.,   *Gilbert and Sullivan and their World* (1973)

BRADLEY, I.,   'Gilbert and Sullivan and the Victorian Age', *History Today*, September 1981

———   *The Complete Annotated Gilbert and Sullivan* (1996)

———   *Oh Joy! Oh Rapture!: The Enduring Phenomenon of Gilbert and Sullivan* (2005)

BRAHMS, C.,   *Gilbert and Sullivan* (1975)

BROWNE, E. A.,   *W. S. Gilbert* (1907)

DARK, S. AND GREY, R., *W. S. Gilbert: His Life and Letters* (1923)

DARLINGTON, W. A., *The World of Gilbert and Sullivan* (1950)

GILBERT, W. S.,   *The Bab Ballads* (1904)

———   *The Savoy Operas: Complete Text of the Gilbert and Sullivan Operas as originally produced in the years 1875-1896* (1926)

HAYTER, C.,   *Gilbert and Sullivan* (1987)

JACOBS, A.,   *Gilbert and Sullivan* (1951)

———   *Arthur Sullivan: A Victorian Musician* (1984)

———   'Sullivan, Sir Arthur Seymour (1842-1900)', *Oxford Dictionary of National Biography* (2004)

PEARSON, H.,   *Gilbert and Sullivan* (1935)

———   *Gilbert, His Life and Strife* (1957)

STEDMAN, J. W.,   *W. S. Gilbert; A Classic Victorian and His Theatre* (1996)

———   'Gilbert, Sir William Schwenk (1836-1911)', *Oxford Dictionary of National Biography* (2004)

WILLIAMSON, A.,   *Gilbert and Sullivan Opera: An Assessment* (1953)

Subject Panels in
Haphazard Sequence

1   The Bab Ballads

The Bab Ballads is a collection of fun verses with sketch illustrations by William Schwenk Gilbert first published in 1869, following closely on the heels of *Alice in Wonderland* (1865) by Lewis Carroll (Charles Lutwidge Dodgson 1832-1898), with its famous illustrations by Sir John Tenniel. However, Gilbert was not copying, as 'Bab' illustrations and their accompanying humorous articles appeared in the early 1860s in *Fun*, a magazine started, under the editorship of actor and playwright Henry James Byron in competition with *Punch* magazine.

The *Bab Ballads* style appears to be a simplified version of the genre developed by George Cruikshank (1792-1878) and John Leech (1817-1864), but its success is probably due in part to the minimalism of the sketches where the simple ink strokes evoke humour in every line and curve. However, the simple strokes are misleading, because for the printing process a wood-block needed to be made where in fact the simple strokes are merely the remnants after the surrounding wood is cut away—a time-consuming and laborious task.

The book takes its title from Gilbert's childhood nickname. He later began to sign his illustrations 'Bab'. Gilbert wrote the 'ballads' collected in the book before he became famous for his comic opera librettos with Arthur Sullivan. In writing these verses Gilbert developed his 'topsy-turvy' style in which the humour is derived by setting up a ridiculous premise and working out its logical consequences, however absurd. The ballads also reveal Gilbert's cynical and satirical approach to humour.

The ballads were famous on their own, as well as being a source for plot elements, characters and songs that Gilbert recycled in the Gilbert and Sullivan operas. They were read aloud at private dinner parties, at public banquets and even in the House of Lords. The ballads have been much published, and some have been recorded or otherwise adapted.

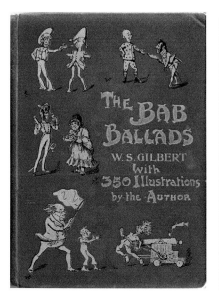 

Left: The front cover of the 1898 edition of *The Bab Ballads* where Gilbert collected together 350 of his creations.

Right: The frontispiece from the first edition of 1868.

2   William Schwenck Gilbert—The Early Years

William Schwenck Gilbert was born in London, only son of William Gilbert (1804-1890) and Anne Mary Bye Morris (1812–1888).

Gilbert senior was orphaned early and was brought up his mother's sister Mary née Mathers (b. 1778) and her husband John Samuel Schwenck (d. 1865), a childless and financially comfortable couple. Gilbert's father had also left him a legacy which could not be accessed until he reached the age of 26. Gilbert served in the East India Company as a midshipman from 1818 to 1821 but being unhappy with the conditions he quit the service, and then spent several years in Italy. He returned to England about 1825 and studied at Guy's Hospital and served as an assistant surgeon in the navy, and then he entered the Royal College of Surgeons in 1830. At this time he received his annuity from his father's estate, giving him financial independence. He gave up his medical career to pursue his interests in literature. He wrote a considerable number of novels, biographies, histories, essays (especially about the dangers of alcohol and the plight of the poor) and popular fantasy stories—mostly in the 1860s and 1870s, some of which were illustrated by his son, William Schwenck.

Gilbert senior married Anne Mary Bye Morris on 14 February 1836 and William Schwenck was born on 18 November 1836 at Anne's parents' house in Southampton Street. In 1838 Gilbert took his wife and toddler son on an extended trip to Italy and France, not returning until 1847. It was during this formative period that the infant William Schwenck—nicknamed 'Babs'—learnt Italian and French (he later kept his diary in French so that the servants could not read it).

In England Gilbert and Anne 'led an increasingly quarrelsome life' in London which caused William Schwenck to live an unhappy childhood. He was educated at Western Grammar School, Brompton, London, and then at the Great Ealing School, where he became head boy and wrote plays for school performances and painted scenery. He then attended King's College London, graduating in 1856. He intended to take the examinations for a commission in the Royal Artillery, but with the end of the Crimean War, fewer recruits were needed, and the only commission available to Gilbert would have been in a line regiment. Instead he joined the Civil Service: he was an assistant clerk in the Privy Council Office for four years and hated it. In 1859 he joined the Militia, a part-time volunteer force formed for the defence of Britain, with which he served until 1878 (in between writing and other work), reaching the rank of Captain. In 1863 he received a bequest of £300 that he used to leave the civil service and take up a brief career as a barrister (he had already entered the Inner Temple as a student), but his legal practice was not successful, averaging just five clients a year.

To supplement his income from 1861 on, Gilbert wrote a variety of stories, skits and theatre reviews many parodying the play being reviewed, and mostly under his childhood pseudonym 'Bab'. He also illustrated poems for several comic magazines, primarily *Fun*, started in 1861 by Henry James Byron. He published stories, articles, and reviews in papers such as *The Cornhill Magazine*, *London Society*, *Tinsley's Magazine* and *Temple Bar: A London Magazine for Town and Country Readers*. In addition, Gilbert was a drama critic for *The Illustrated London News* and in the 1860s he also contributed to Tom Hood's Christmas annuals and other publications. The poems, illustrated humorously by Gilbert, proved immensely popular and were reprinted in book form as *The Bab Ballads*. He later returned to many of these as source material for his plays and comic operas.

In 1867 Gilbert married Lucy Agnes Turner (1847-1936), whom he called 'Kitty'. She was the daughter of Thomas Metcalfe Blois Turner (1809-1847) and Herbertina Compton (1815-1913). Lucy's father had died at Bombay in July 1847, three months before her birth. Her mother, Herbertina was the daughter of Sir Herbert Compton who became Lord Chief Justice of Bombay and was knighted in 1831.

The marriage of William Schwenck and Lucy Agnes appears to have been happy, but they were childless. He wrote many affectionate letters to her over the years and they were socially active in London often holding dinner parties.

Opposite page, left: William Schwenck Gilbert *c.* 1864.

Opposite page, right: Lucy *c.* 1870.

Right: An early photograph of W. S. Gilbert in military uniform with tartan breeches, probably not part of his militia uniform, but the reason behind the photograph is not apparent.

3   *Arthur Seymour Sullivan—The Early Years*

Arthur Seymour Sullivan (1842-1900), was born at Lambeth, Surrey, (now London), second son of the only two surviving children of Thomas Sullivan (1805-1866) and Mary Clementina Sullivan, née Coghlan (1811- 82). His father was a military bandmaster, clarinettist and music teacher, born in Ireland and raised at Chelsea, London; his mother was born at Great Marlow, Buckinghamshire, daughter of Irish-born James Coghlan (1780-1824), and Italian-born Mary Louisa Margaret Righi (1786-1829).

Through his father's influence, Arthur could play many of the instruments in the military band by the age of eight. He was to say later:

> I was intensely interested in all that the band did, and learned to play every wind instrument, with which I formed not merely a passing acquaintance, but a real, life-long, intimate friendship. I gradually learned the peculiarities of each ... what it could do and what it was unable to do. I learned in the best possible way how to write for an orchestra.

Arthur Sullivan as chorister of the Chapel Royal, *c.* 1855.

His precocious talent was recognised and in April 1854 he was accepted—although at nearly twelve he was over the usual age—as one of the child choristers of the Chapel Royal. Here he came under the tutelage of the Revd Thomas Helmore and quickly became a favourite choice when solos were required and was promoted to 'first boy' in 1856. In the summer of that same year, Sullivan, despite being the youngest entrant, won the competition for the first Mendelssohn Scholarship. This enabled him to study at the Royal Academy of Music, where his tutors included Sir William Sterndale Bennett (1816-75) and Sir John Goss (1800-80)—whose own teacher, Thomas Attwood, had been a pupil of Mozart, and then from 1858 at the Conservatory in Leipzig, at that time the finest musical training school in the world. Here he learned from the best teachers in Europe, including Ignaz Moscheles (1794-1870), Moritz Hauptmann (1792-1868), Julius Rietz (1812-77) and Louis Plaidy (1810-74). He was trained in Mendelssohn's ideas and techniques but was also exposed to a variety of styles, including those of Schubert, Verdi, Bach and Wagner. Visiting a synagogue, he was so struck by some of the cadences and progressions of the music that thirty years later he could recall them for use in his grand opera, *Ivanhoe*. He became friendly with the future impresario Carl Rosa and the violinist Joseph Joachim, among others.

Sullivan left Leipzig in April 1861 after a successful performance of his final examination piece, a set of incidental music to Shakespeare's *The Tempest*. Back in London he took work as a church organist and taught to earn his living. In April 1862 *The Tempest* was performed at one of the celebrated Crystal Palace Saturday concerts and was an immediate and enormous success, so much so that a repeat performance had to be given the following week. This second performance was highly praised by Charles Dickens. Almost overnight the precocious young man was making his name and *The Musical Times* described it as a 'sensation'. He began building a reputation as England's most promising young composer.

Left: Arthur Sullivan in his Royal Academy of Music uniform, 8 September 1858.

Right: A studio photograph of a nonchalant Arthur Sullivan at the age of 22, with his stove pipe hat upside-down on the chair he is leaning against *c.* 1864, probably a photograph by Oliver Sarony, a Quebecois/American photographer.

4   Frederic Emes Clay

Frederic Emes Clay (1838-1889) was born in Paris, son of James Clay, a British MP, and his wife, Eliza Camilla Woolrych. He commenced his working career as a clerk at the Treasury, but after the death of his father his inheritance enabled him to become a full-time composer and most of his compositions were written for the stage. His first professionally produced piece was an opera entitled *Court and Cottage*, with a libretto by Tom Taylor, which was produced at Covent Garden Theatre in 1862. In 1865, for the same theatre, he composed another opera, the unsuccessful *Constance* (1865), with a libretto by Thomas William Robertson. With W. S. Gilbert he wrote *Ages Ago* (1869) for Thomas German Reed's performance venue, The Royal Gallery of Illustration, located at 14 Regent Street. This piece ran for 350 performances and was revived several times. Clay introduced Gilbert to Arthur Sullivan during a rehearsal for *Ages Ago*. This was followed by *The Gentleman in Black* (1870, also with Gilbert), *In Possession* (1871, libretto by Robert Reece), *Happy Arcadia* (1872, with Gilbert), *Oriana* (1873, libretto by James Albery), *Green Old Age* and *Cattarina* (both 1874, libretti by Robert Reece), *Princess Toto* (1875, the last collaboration between Clay and Gilbert), and *Don Quixote* (1876, libretto by Harry Paulton and Alfred Maltby).

Ages Ago (a one-act piece) and *Princess Toto* (a three-act comic opera) are considered to be among Clay's most tuneful and attractive works. *The Times* wrote that the music of *Princess Toto* 'is probably surpassed by no modern English work of the kind for gaiety and melodious charm'.

After conducting the second performance of a later piece, *The Golden Ring*, in December 1883, Clay suffered a stroke that paralysed him and cut short his productive life. In 1889 at the age of 51, he was found drowned in his bath at the home of his sisters in Great Marlow, Buckinghamshire, presumably by suicide. He was buried in Brompton cemetery.

Left: Frederic Clay, Hon. Seymour 'Sim' Egerton (1839-1898), later, 4th earl of Wilton, and Arthur Sullivan, *c.* 1868.

Right: The front cover for sheet music from *Don Quixote*.

5   Clerkenwell Sessions House

The Middlesex Sessions House, (as it was originally known), was designed by the Middlesex County surveyor, Thomas Rogers. The building was built from 1779-82 and was used as a courthouse from 1782 until 1920. The building consisted of two large court rooms, dungeons for holding prisoners, and a grand living space for the resident judges. In its day, Middlesex Sessions House had a reputation for being one of the harshest courthouses in the country. Justice meant punishment and sentences were notoriously severe. A 78-year-old woman once received seven years for stealing a joint of meat. It was at Clerkenwell Sessions House that Gilbert commenced his short legal career.

The building was designed in the grand Romanesque style favoured during the reign of King George III. In 1860 a new courtroom was built above the entrance. The Sessions House served as the main judicial and administrative centre for Middlesex until 1889, when Middlesex County Council and London County Council were created. The Sessions House became property of London County Council during the subsequent division of assets. The Old Sessions House held its last court case in 1920 and was subsequently sold.

Clerkenwell Sessions House. *Wikimedia Commons, photo: Steve Cadman via Flickr*

The principal court-room in 1914. *British History Online*

6   Nelly Bromley

Eleanor Elizabeth Emily (Nelly) Bromley (1850-1939) was famous for having created the role of the Plaintiff in Gilbert and Sullivan's first success, *Trial by Jury*, although she played in that piece for just over three months. She was born in Southwark, Surrey to an actress and singer, also Eleanor Bromley (1826-1860) and an unknown father. After her mother's death, Eleanor and her younger half-sister, Jessy Cook, were raised by their grandmother Hannah. She used her nickname 'Nelly' as her stage name and began a stage career in her teens. By December 1866, she was acting at the Royalty Theatre in London, playing Dolly Mayflower in a burlesque by F. C. Burnand of *Black-Eyed Susan*. She remained in the company at the Royalty, acting in other burlesques, including W. S. Gilbert's *Highly Improbable* and as Nimble Ned in Burnand's burlesque on Claude Duval. She soon appeared in many of the West End theatres. By 1873, she had become popular in H. B. Farnie's musical comedies. She then returned to the Royalty under the management of Richard D'Oyly Carte acting for Selina Dolaro (1849-1889), a singer, actress, theatre manager, to create the role of 'the Plaintiff', on 25 March 1875, in Gilbert and Sullivan's *Trial by Jury*. Although Eleanor was a critical success in the part, she left the production in July 1875. 'Trial by Jury Lancers', Charles D'Albert's dance arrangement of numbers from the piece, was dedicated to her.

Left and right: Two studio photographs of Eleanor 'Nelly' Bromley.

She next played at the Criterion Theatre as Mrs Graham in *The Great Divorce Case*. Later in 1875 she played the Princess of Granada in H. S. Leigh's translation of Jacques Offenbach's *Les brigands*, presented at the Globe Theatre with the title *Falsacappa*. She acted regularly at the Criterion in a series of long-running English adaptations of French farces. By 1881, Eleanor had moved in with artist Archibald Stuart-Wortley (1849-1905). They married in 1884, and he acted as father to her four children: Lillian Bertha (1870-1904), Zoe (1871-1948), Valentine Robert (1878-1950) and John (1880-1918), killed in action, Bullecourt, France; their fathers are unknown. In 1882, she replaced Lottie Venne in Burnand's farce *Betsy* at the Criterion. In 1883, she appeared in *Freedom* at the Theatre Royal, Drury Lane, earning a good review in *The Theatre*. She retired from the stage about this time. In later life, Eleanor used her married name, Mrs Archibald Stuart-Wortley.

Left: The front cover to the music *Trial by Jury Lancers*, by Charles D'Albert; dance arrangement of songs from *Trial by Jury*.

Right: Archibald Stuart-Wortley (1849-1905), painter and illustrator, youngest son of James Stuart-Wortley, 1st Baron Wharncliffe. A caricature by 'Spy', Leslie Ward (1851-1922), and published in *Vanity Fair*, 18 January 1890. Stuart-Wortley was the lover and later the husband of Nelly Bromley.

7 Cox and Box

Cox and Box, is a one-act comic opera with a libretto by F. C. Burnand and music by Arthur Sullivan, based on the 1847 farce *Box and Cox* by John Maddison Morton, featuring the characters John Box, a journeyman printer, James Cox, a journeyman hatter and Mrs Bouncer. It was Sullivan's first successful comic opera. The story concerns a landlord who lets a room to two lodgers, one who works at night and one who works during the day. When one of them has the day off, they meet each other in the room and tempers flare. Sullivan wrote this piece five years before his first opera with W. S. Gilbert, *Thespis*.

The piece premiered in 1866 and was seen a few times at charity benefits in 1867. Once given a professional production in 1869, it became popular, running for 264 performances and enjoying many revivals and further charity performances.

Above left: Sheet music front page for the quadrille, based on Sullivan's operetta *Cox and Box*.
Above: Disraeli (left) and Gladstone depicted as Box and Cox, *Punch*, 19 February 1870.
Left: Francis Cowley Burnand, from *Vanity Fair*, 8 January 1881.
Below: Detail from a *Cox and Box* advertising poster.

8   Frederic Sullivan

Frederic Sullivan (1837-1877), Arthur's elder brother, trained as an architectural draftsman but soon decided on a career as a performer. He later quipped—'and I still draw large houses'. In 1871, he first performed the role of Mr Cox in a revival of his brother's first comic opera, *Cox and Box*, and later that year created the role of Apollo in the first Gilbert and Sullivan opera, *Thespis*. In 1874 Fred met and became firm friends with George Grossmith. Later in 1874, he appeared at the Opera Comique as Mercury in *Ixion Rewheel'd*, an opéra bouffe extravaganza by F. C. Burnand, and at the Holborn Amphitheatre as the impoverished and henpecked Duke of Rodomont, in *Melusine the Enchantress* by G. M. Layton and Hervé. In 1875, Fred created the role of the Learned Judge in *Trial by Jury*—a piece specifically written for him by Gilbert and Sullivan, and he also played in the accompanying Offenbach piece, *La Périchole*, and earning enthusiastic reviews. The first-night critics reserved especial praise for his performance: 'The greatest "hit" was made by Mr F. Sullivan, whose blending of official dignity, condescension, and, at the right moment, extravagant humour, made the character of the Judge stand out with all requisite prominence, and added much to the interest of the piece.' The critic for *The Times* agreed: 'Mr. F. Sullivan's impersonation of the learned and impressionable Judge deserves a special word of praise for its quiet and natural humour.' F. C. Burnand wrote of him: 'Fred Sullivan, Arthur's brother, was one of the most naturally comic little men I ever came across. He, too, was a first-rate practical musician.... As he was the most absurd person, so was he the very kindliest. The brothers were devoted to each other'.

Fred then toured in *Trial*, and French operettas, returning to London for the revival of *Trial*. By early 1876 his health was deteriorating and he died of liver disease and tuberculosis at the early age 39 leaving a pregnant widow and seven young children. After Fred's death, Arthur became guardian to the children and helped support Fred's family for the rest of his life.

Left: A photo of Fred Sullivan in an early role.

Centre: Publicity photograph of Fred Sullivan taken *c.* 1870.

Right: Fred Sullivan as the Learned Judge in *Trial by Jury, c.* 1875.

9   The Savoy Theatre and the D'Oyly Carte Opera Company

The site of the Savoy Theatre was original land granted to Count Piero of Savoy, the maternal uncle of Eleanor of Provence, queen-consort of Henry III (1216-1272), who accompanied her to London. The palace on the site was burned down by Wat Tyler's followers in the Peasants' Revolt of 1381 and the site later became a hospital. The remaining building burned down in 1864 and the site lay empty until bought by Richard D'Oyly Carte in 1880 to build the Savoy Theatre specifically for the production of the Gilbert and Sullivan operas. Due to problems with officialdom and builders, the advertised opening date had to be put back several times and the Savoy finally opened on 10 October 1881. Carte had at one time intended to call it the Beaufort Theatre, but he announced in a letter to *The Daily Telegraph* in 1881, 'On the Savoy Manor there was formerly a theatre. I have used the ancient name as an appropriate title for the present one'. The exterior of the building was made from red brick and Portland stone. The interior decoration was 'in the manner of the Italian Renaissance', with white, pale yellow and gold predominating, including a gold satin curtain, red boxes and dark blue seats. There were none of the cherubs, deities and mythical creatures familiar from the décor of rival theatres. Carte wanted nothing that would appear too garish or gaudy to his target, middle-class audience.

Reporting on the opening night *The Times* commented, 'A perfect view of the stage can be had from every seat in the house'. There were three tiers with four levels: stalls and pit, balcony, circle, and amphitheatre and gallery at the top. The total seating capacity was 1,292. The theatre originally had its main entrance on the Embankment. The parcel on which it was built is steep, stretching from the Strand down to the Embankment along Beaufort Street. After Carte built the Savoy Hotel in 1889, the theatre entrance was moved to its present location at the hotel's courtyard off the Strand. The Savoy was a state-of-the-art theatre and the first public building to be lit entirely by electricity. Carte later wrote: 'The greatest drawbacks to the enjoyment of the theatrical performances are, undoubtedly, the foul air and heat which pervade all theatres. As everyone knows, each gas-burner consumes as much oxygen as many people, and causes great heat beside. The incandescent lamps consume no oxygen, and cause no perceptible heat'.

The original façade of the Savoy Theatre, 1881.

Original interior of Savoy Theatre, 1881.

Carte and his manager, George Edwardes introduced several innovations including numbered seating, free programme booklets, good quality whisky in the bars, and a policy of no tipping for cloakroom or other services.

The work that opened the new theatre was Gilbert and Sullivan's comic opera *Patience*, which had been running since April 1881 at the smaller Opera Comique. The last eight of Gilbert and Sullivan's comic operas were premièred at the Savoy: *Iolanthe* (1882), *Princess Ida* (1884), *The Mikado* (1885), *Ruddigore* (1887), *The Yeomen of the Guard* (1888) *The Gondoliers* (1889), *Utopia, Limited* (1893), and *The Grand Duke* (1896).

Following D'Oyly Carte's death in 1901 the theatre closed in 1903, and re-opened under new management in 1904. In 1915 D'Oyly Carte's son, Rupert, took over the management. After serving in the Royal Navy in the First World War, Carte decided to bring the D'Oyly Carte Opera Company back to London in first-rate style. In early 1929 he closed the Savoy Theatre, and the interior was completely rebuilt. It reopened on 21 October 1929 with a new production of *The Gondoliers* designed by Charles Ricketts and conducted by Malcolm Sargent. There were Gilbert and Sullivan seasons at the Savoy Theatre in 1929-30, 1932-33, 1951, 1954, 1961-62, 1975, 2000, 2001, 2002 and 2003. After Rupert D'Oyly Carte's death in 1948 his daughter, Bridget succeeded to the Company and became a director and later president of the Savoy Hotel group, which controlled the theatre. Dame Bridget died childless in 1985, bringing the family line to an end.

While the theatre was being renovated in February 1990, a fire gutted the building, except for the stage and backstage areas. It was restored as faithfully as possible to the 1929 designs. In 2000 the briefly reconstituted D'Oyly Carte Opera Company produced *H.M.S. Pinafore* at the theatre, followed by a second D'Oyly Carte season, playing *The Pirates of Penzance*. In 2002 there was a season of D'Oyly Carte productions of *Iolanthe*, *The Yeomen of the Guard* and *The Mikado*. The Savoy Hotel group, including the theatre, was sold in 2004 and has subsequently passed through several corporate hands.

10   George Grossmith—Part 1

George Grossmith (1847-1912), was born at Islington, London, eldest son of George Grossmith (1820-1880), and his wife Louisa Emmeline Weedon (1826-1882). His father was the chief reporter for *The Times* at the Bow Street Magistrates' Court and was also a lecturer and entertainer. George had one sister, Emily (1850-1859), and one brother, Walter Weedon (1852-1919), of whom more later.

Grossmith had hoped to become a barrister. Instead, he worked for many years, beginning in the 1860s, training and then substituting for his father as the Bow Street reporter for *The Times*, among other publications. In 1873, Grossmith married Emmeline Rosa Noyce (1849-1905) and they had four children: George (1874-1935), Sylvia (1875-1932), Lawrence (1877-1944) and Cordelia Rosa (1879-1943).

Grossmith received some recognition for amateur songs and sketches at private parties and then took to the stage in 1870 with a sketch called *Human Oddities*, written by his father, and a song called 'The Gay (i.e. carefree) Photographer'. All of his early work was written by himself and his father.

In 1874 Grossmith met and became firm friends with Fred Sullivan, and afterwards, he met Sullivan's brother Arthur and impresario Richard D'Oyly Carte. Through these connections he began to be invited to entertain at private 'society' parties, which he continued to do throughout his career. Later, these parties would often occur late in the evening after Grossmith performed at the Savoy Theatre.

Left: Carte de Visite of George Grossmith and Emmeline Rosa Grossmith by Robert W. Thrupp, Birmingham, *c.* 1875.

Right: George Grossmith out of costume. A studio photograph *c.* 1877.

Left: A classic George Grossmith grin, a studio photograph of Grossmith as The Lord Chancellor in *Iolanthe* by Elliott and Fry, 55 & 56 Baker Street in London, *c.* 1877.

Right: Grossmith in the character of Sir Joseph Porter.

Following Fred Sullivan's early decline and death in 1877 from liver disease and tuberculosis, Gilbert and Sullivan sought a leading man. In November 1877 Grossmith received a letter from Arthur Sullivan inviting him to take a part in his new piece with W. S. Gilbert: *The Sorcerer.* Grossmith had appeared in charity performances of *Trial by Jury*, where both Sullivan and Gilbert had seen him. After singing for Sullivan, upon meeting Gilbert, Grossmith wondered aloud if the role shouldn't be played by 'a fine man with a fine voice'. Gilbert replied, 'That is exactly what we don't want.' Although Grossmith had reservations about cancelling his touring engagements and going into the 'wicked' professional theatre, and Richard D'Oyly Carte's backers objected to casting a sketch comedian in the central role of a comic opera, Grossmith was hired. Notwithstanding his own and D'Oyly Carte's reservations, Grossmith became a great hit as the tradesman-like John Wellington Wells, the title role in *The Sorcerer*, and became a regular member of Richard D'Oyly Carte's company. He created all nine of the lead comic baritone roles in Gilbert and Sullivan's Savoy Operas in London from 1877 to 1889, including the pompous First Lord of the Admiralty, Sir Joseph Porter, in *H.M.S. Pinafore* (1878); Major-General Stanley in *The Pirates of Penzance*, who is an expert at everything except 'military knowledge' (1880); the aesthetic poet, Reginald Bunthorne in *Patience* (1881); the love-lonely Lord Chancellor in *Iolanthe* (1882); the sarcastic cripple, King Gama, in *Princess Ida* (1884); Ko-Ko the cheap tailor, elevated to the post of Lord High Executioner, in *The Mikado* (1885); the accursed Robin Oakapple in *Ruddigore* (1887); and the pathetic jester, Jack Point, in *The Yeomen of the Guard* (1888).

11   W. H. Smith—First Lord of the Admiralty

William Henry Smith (1825-1891), was born in London, the son of strict Methodists William Henry Smith (1792-1865) and his wife, Mary Ann Cooper (1792-1851). He joined the business in 1846, at which time the firm became W. H. Smith & Son. He had, at the age of 16, expressed a wish to go to Oxford, but, in deference to his father's wishes, he entered the news-agency house in the Strand and became his father's partner. The elder Smith had secured the position of leading newsagent in the country, but his strength was failing, and the management passed gradually into his son's hands. The development of railways afforded an opportunity which Smith was not slow to seize. Although his father resented any attempt to extend the enterprise beyond that of an agency for the sale of newspapers, the son opened negotiations with the different railway companies for the right to erect bookstalls at their stations, and in 1851 secured a monopoly on the London and North-Western system. Taking scrupulous care to exclude pernicious literature which had previously made these bookstalls notorious, young Smith got the name of 'the North-Western Missionary,' and by 1862 this reputation had secured for the firm the exclusive right of selling books and newspapers on all the important railways. The repeal of the newspaper stamp duty in 1854 gave an enormous impetus, and W. H. Smith & Son were in a position to derive immediate advantage from it. The Great Exhibition of 1851 had introduced open-air advertisement. Smith was first in the field, securing a lease of the blank walls in all the principal railway stations.

Left: William Henry Smith, depicted in *Vanity Fair*, 9 March 1872.

Right: *Punch*, 13 October 1877, cartoon by John Tenniel (1820-1914).

Left: William Henry Smith, 1883, engraved by John Douglas Miller (1860-1903), after a painting by George Richmond (1809-1896).

Centre: A photo of a bristle-cheeked W. H. Smith autographed by himself on Guy Fawkes's Day, 5 November 1885.

Right: A greyer-cheeked W. H. Smith depicted in *Vanity Fair*, 12 November 1887.

Smith perhaps owed his first approach to the Conservative party to his rejection as a candidate for election to the Reform Club in 1862. He stood for Westminster in 1865 as a Liberal-Conservative, but was left at the bottom of the poll; but in 1868, with the franchise having been extended to householders in boroughs he was returned to parliament for the same constituency. The expenditure on the election had been enormous. Smith's return was petitioned against, and the indiscretion of his agents proved well-nigh fatal to his retaining the seat; but, as *The Times* observed in a leader on the verdict, 'a good character has, to Mr Smith at any rate, proved better than riches. It may be a question whether the latter won the seat for him, but there can be no question that the former has saved it.'

In 1874 Disraeli appointed Smith to the post of financial secretary to the Treasury. In 1877, he became first lord of the Admiralty. Smith's appointment was the inspiration for the character of Sir Joseph Porter, KCB, in *H.M.S. Pinafore*. Gilbert had written to Sullivan in December 1877 'The fact that the First Lord in the opera is a Radical of the most pronounced type will do away with any suspicion that W. H. Smith is intended.' However, the character was seen as a reflection on Smith and even Disraeli was overheard to refer to his first lord as 'Pinafore Smith'.

In 1885, Smith served as chief secretary for Ireland. He was twice secretary of state for war, the first time during Lord Salisbury's brief ministry between 1885 and 1886, and the second when the Conservatives won the 1886 General Election. He succeeded this appointment in 1887 as first lord of the Treasury and leader of the House of Commons, and became Lord Warden of the Cinque Ports in 1891.

12   George Grossmith—Part 2

In 1883, *The Times*, reviewing a performance of *Iolanthe*, wrote: 'Mr. Grossmith's impersonation of the Lord Chancellor has ... become an exquisitely refined satire.' On the other hand, his sketch comedy background had trained him to improvise comic business leading to an exchange with Gilbert during rehearsals for *The Mikado* about an improvised moment in which Jessie Bond pushed him as they kneeled before the Mikado, and he rolled completely over. Gilbert requested that they cut it out, and Grossmith replied: 'but I get an enormous laugh by it'. Gilbert replied 'So you would if you sat on a pork-pie.'

One interesting facet of Grossmith's career is his nervousness and his compensatory drug-taking. He was noted for being jittery on opening nights and Arthur Sullivan wrote afterwards, 'All went very well except Grossmith, whose nervousness nearly upset the piece'. Even after he had given thousands of stage appearances he feared he would forget his lines. He also suffered badly from insomnia. It is not unlikely that he took morphine or cocaine to calm himself or to boost his self-confidence. His lack of confidence was not helped where the company was being driven ruthlessly by Gilbert. Though Gilbert can hardly be held responsible for Grossmith's nerves, it was partly due to the extreme methods of the producer that the actor took to drugs in order to keep himself going; and at the end of his long engagement at the Savoy Theatre a member of the company was horrified by the sight of Grossmith's punctured arms. It is said that when he died in 1912 the coroner at the inquest mentioned that the arm was bruised from needle punctures. However, no report of the inquest has been located. Many drugs were readily available in late nineteenth-century and Edwardian England, and were sold without legal controls.

Left: A representation of Grossmith as Major-General Stanley.

Right: George (right) with his brother Weedon, 1897. From this unsmiling photograph it is difficult to believe they could have co-written the highly amusing *Diary of a Nobody*.

Left: George Grossmith by 'Spy' in *Vanity Fair*, 21 January 1888, entitled 'The Pinafore'.

Centre: George Grossmith in the character of Jack Point, in *The Yeomen of the Guard*, 1889.

Right: George Grossmith with his piano—his best friend.

Grossmith left the D'Oyly Carte Opera Company near the end of the original run of *The Yeomen of the Guard* on 17 August 1889 and resumed his career entertaining at the piano, which he continued to do for more than fifteen years afterwards. Despite his dislike of travelling, he toured in Britain, Ireland, and America. His drawing-room sketches included his own popular songs. According to *The Times*, 'His genial satire was enjoyed even by those at whom its shafts were aimed.' When he toured Scotland in the autumn of 1890, Grossmith gave a command performance for Queen Victoria at Balmoral Castle. He also composed the music for a three-act comic opera with a libretto by Gilbert, *Haste to the Wedding* (1892). In this piece, his son George Grossmith Jr made his stage debut. Musically more challenging than any composition he had attempted before, this work was unsuccessful. Later, however, Grossmith said that the experience of writing with Gilbert was one of the happiest of his life.

In 1892, Grossmith collaborated with his brother Weedon to expand a series of columns they had written in 1888-89 for *Punch*. *The Diary of a Nobody* was published as a novel and has never been out of print since. The book is a sharp analysis of social insecurity, and Charles Pooter was immediately recognised as one of the great comic characters of English literature.

Grossmith had become the most popular solo entertainer of his day, and his tours earned him far more than he had earned while performing with the D'Oyly Carte Opera Company. He suffered from depression after the death of his wife in 1905, and his health began to fail so that he increasingly missed engagements. He was nevertheless persuaded to continue giving his entertainments, which he did on a less frequent basis, until November 1908. The following year he retired to Folkestone, where he died at the age of 64 in 1912. The obituary in *The Times* noted Grossmith's 'nimbleness, his diverting tricks, his still more diverting dignity—the dignity of a man of few inches high or round—and his incomparable power of rapid speech and singing.' *The Daily Telegraph* wrote of his Jack Point: 'Whether giving expression to poor Jack's professional wit, or hiding a sorry heart behind light words... Mr Grossmith was master of the part he assumed.'

13   *Prince George, duke of Cambridge*

Prince George (1819-1904) was the eldest son of Prince Adolphus, duke of Cambridge, and Princess Augusta of Hesse-Kassel. His father was the seventh son of King George III. He embarked upon a military career initially in the Hanoverian Army and then in 1837, in the British Army. Inevitably—due to his pedigree—he rose through the ranks.

In February 1854 Cambridge received command of the 1st Division of the British Army in the East. He was present at the battles of the Alma, Balaclava and Inkerman, and at the siege of Sebastopol. On 5 July 1856, he was appointed general commanding-in-chief, retitled field marshal commanding-in-chief on 9 November 1862 and commander-in-chief of the forces on 20 November 1887. He earned a reputation for being resistant to change, making promotions based upon an officer's social standing, rather than merit. He rebuked one of his more intelligent subordinates with the words: 'Brains? I don't believe in brains! You haven't any, I know, Sir!' He was equally forthright in his reluctance to adopt change: 'There is a time for everything, and the time for change is when you can no longer help it.' Following the Prussian victory in the 1870-71 Franco-Prussian War, William Gladstone and secretary of state for war Edward Cardwell called for the Army to undergo major reforms. Cardwell succeeded in pushing a number through, including one that made the commander-in-chief nominally report to the secretary of state for war. The duke was opposed to most reforms because they struck at the heart of his view of the Army. According to one source, he 'stoutly resisted almost every attempt at reform or modernization'. Parliament passed the War Office Act 1870, which formally subordinated the commander-in-chief to the secretary of state and abolished the custom of purchasing an office. The duke of Cambridge strongly resented this move, a sentiment shared by many officers, who would no longer be able to sell their commissions. The duke was forced to resign his post in 1895, and was succeeded by Lord Wolseley.

Left: Collodion of Prince George, 1855, by Roger Fenton.

Right: HRH Prince George, duke of Cambridge, by Francis Montague Holl. *Royal Collection*

14   Edward Cardwell

Edward Cardwell, 1st Viscount Cardwell (1813-1886), was born at Pendleton, Lancashire. He was educated at Oxford, and the Inner Temple, where he was called to the bar in 1838. After a career in the Colonial Office he was elected MP in 1842. He supported Sir Robert Peel and after the Conservative split in 1846 over the Corn Laws, Cardwell followed Peel, and became a member of the Peelite faction, later moving to the Liberals. When Gladstone returned to power in 1868 he was appointed as secretary of state for war. In what became known as the 'Cardwell reforms', he reorganised the Army, introduced professional standards for officers—including advancement by merit rather than purchase.

In 1870 Gladstone and Cardwell pushed through Parliament major changes in Army organisation. Germany's triumph over France proved that the Prussian system of professional soldiers was far superior to the traditional system of gentlemen-soldiers that Britain used. The reforms were not radical and Gladstone seized the moment to enact them. The goal was to centralise the power of the War Office, abolish purchase of commissions, and create reserve forces stationed in Britain by establishing short terms of service for enlisted men. In 1868 Cardwell abolished flogging, raising the private soldier status to more like an honourable career. In 1870 he abolished 'bounty money' for recruits, and pulled 20,000 soldiers out of self-governing colonies.

The bill, which would have compensated current owners for their cash investments, passed the Commons in 1871 but was blocked by the Lords. Gladstone then moved to drop the system without any reimbursements, forcing the Lords to backtrack. Liberals rallied to Gladstone's anti-elitism, pointing to the case of Lord Cardigan (1797-1868), who spent £40,000 for his commission and proved incompetent in the Crimean war, where he led the disastrous 'Charge of the Light Brigade' at the Battle of Balaklava in 1854. Cardwell's final success was in making the office of secretary of state for war superior to the Army's commander-in-chief; the commander was the duke of Cambridge, the Queen's first cousin, and an opponent of any reforms.

Left: Edward Cardwell, 1st Viscount Cardwell, a portrait from 1871 by George Richmond (d. 1896). *National Portrait Gallery*

Right: Cardwell caricatured by 'Ape' in *Vanity Fair*, 3 April 1869.

15   William Gladstone

William Ewart Gladstone (1809-1898), was born in Liverpool to Scottish parents. He first entered the House of Commons in 1832, beginning his political career in a grouping which became the Conservative Party under Robert Peel in 1834. Gladstone served as a minister in both of Peel's governments, and in 1846 joined the breakaway Peelite faction, which eventually merged into the new Liberal Party in 1859. He was chancellor under Lord Aberdeen (1852-1855), Lord Palmerston (1859-1865) and Lord Russell (1865-1866). Gladstone's own political doctrine—which emphasised equality of opportunity, free trade, and laissez-faire economic policies—came to be known as Gladstonian liberalism. His popularity amongst the working-class earned him the sobriquet 'The People's William'.

In 1868, Gladstone became prime minister for the first time. Many reforms were passed during his first ministry, including the disestablishment of the Church of Ireland and the introduction of secret voting. After electoral defeat in 1874, Gladstone resigned as leader of the Liberal Party. From 1876 he began a comeback based on opposition to Turkey's reaction to the Bulgarian April Uprising. After the 1880 general election, Gladstone formed his second ministry (1880–1885), which saw the passage of the Third Reform Act as well as crises in Egypt and Ireland, where his government passed repressive measures but also improved the legal rights of Irish tenant farmers. In early 1886, Gladstone proposed home rule for Ireland but was defeated in the House of Commons. The resulting split in the Liberal Party helped keep them out of office—with one short break—for 20 years. Gladstone formed his last government in 1892. The Second Home Rule Bill passed through the Commons but was defeated in the House of Lords in 1893. Gladstone left office in March 1894, aged 84, as the oldest person to serve as prime minister.

Gladstone's cabinet of 1868, by Lowes Cato Dickinson (1819-1908). Edward Cardwell, secretary of state for war is standing, fifth from the right. *National Portrait Gallery*

16   *Benjamin Disraeli*

Benjamin Disraeli, 1st earl of Beaconsfield (1804-1881), was born at Bloomsbury, Middlesex. After several unsuccessful attempts, Disraeli entered the House of Commons in 1837. In 1846 the prime minister at the time, Sir Robert Peel, split the party over his proposal to repeal the Corn Laws, which involved ending the tariff on imported grain. Disraeli clashed with Peel in the House of Commons, and gradually became a major figure in the party. When Lord Derby, the party leader, thrice formed governments in the 1850s and 1860s, Disraeli served as chancellor of the Exchequer and leader of the House of Commons. Upon Derby's retirement in 1868, Disraeli became prime minister briefly before losing that year's general election. He returned to the Opposition, before leading the party to winning a majority in the 1874 general election. He maintained a close friendship with Queen Victoria, who in 1876 appointed him earl of Beaconsfield. Disraeli's second term was dominated by the Eastern Question—the slow decay of the Ottoman Empire and the desire of other European powers, such as Russia, to gain at its expense. Disraeli arranged for the British to purchase a major interest in the Suez Canal Company (in Ottoman-controlled Egypt). In 1878, faced with Russian victories against the Ottomans, he worked at the Congress of Berlin to obtain peace in the Balkans at terms favourable to Britain and unfavourable to Russia, its longstanding enemy. This diplomatic victory over Russia established Disraeli as one of Europe's leading statesmen. World events thereafter moved against the Conservatives. Controversial wars in Afghanistan and South Africa undermined his public support. He angered British farmers by refusing to reinstitute the Corn Laws in response to poor harvests and cheap imported grain. With Gladstone conducting a massive speaking campaign, his Liberals beat Disraeli's Conservatives at the 1880 general election. In his final months, Disraeli led the Conservatives in Opposition.

It should be added as a tailpiece that Disraeli apparently enjoyed the Savoy operas, especially *H.M.S. Pinafore!*

Left: Earl of Beaconsfield KG, photographed at Osborne by Command of HM the Queen, 22 July 1878. Photograph by Cornelius Jabez Hughes. *Harvard Art Museum*

Right: Benjamin Disraeli, Lord Beaconsfield, by John Everett Millais 1881. *National Portrait Gallery*

17   The Missing Budget Box!

George Ward Hunt (1825-1877) entered the House of Commons in 1857 as MP for Northamptonshire North. He was a secretary to the Treasury from 1866 to 1868, in the ministry of the 14th earl of Derby. He was then appointed to the Exchequer when Disraeli took office. By repute, when he presented his one and only Budget speech to parliament he discovered that he had left the ministerial 'Red Box' containing it at home. This is said to be the start of the tradition that, when a chancellor leaves for the House of Commons on Budget Day, he shows the assembled crowd the box by holding it aloft.

Hunt was appointed to the Admiralty for Disraeli's second ministry, serving from 1874 until his death from gout in 1877. Hunt is not relevant to Gilbert & Sullivan other than the fact that his death enabled W. H. Smith to step into his shoes at the Admiralty, but the humorous budget box fiasco would have been precisely the type of ministerial incompetence that would have appealed to Gilbert.

Left: George Ward Hunt, 1873.

Right: Hunt as caricatured by Carlo Pellegrini in *Vanity Fair*, 11 March 1871. The caption on the page reads: 'The fat of the land'.

18   *George Grossmith as John Wellington Wells*

Grossmith was possibly most photographed as John Wellington Wells, of J. W. Wells & Co., Family Sorcerers in *The Sorcerer*. On his work for D'Oyly Carte one biographer has written:

> The agility and droll dignity of his small frame, his dry humour, his pleasant voice, and the skill in rapid enunciation which caused his "patter-songs" to be made a regular feature of these operas, suited Grossmith perfectly to this form of dramatic and musical art.

By contrast, Gilbert expressed this opinion to Sullivan: '[Grossmith] is a d—d bad actor, but he has worked very hard for us, and has endeavoured in every way to meet our wishes during the thirteen years of his engagement.' Gilbert was a notoriously hard task-master and if audience responses were to be judged by he was wrong. Clearly was less than appreciative even if he did reluctantly acknowledge that has Grossmith worked very hard.

Far left: A poster for *The Sorcerer*, 1877.

Left, below left and right: Grossmith as John Wellington Wells in The Sorcerer. Photographs by Herbert Rose Barraud *c.* 1884.

19   *Lord Chelmsford and the Anglo-Zulu War*

Frederic Augustus Thesiger, 2nd Baron Chelmsford (1827-1905), was the eldest child of Frederic Thesiger, a lawyer who became lord chancellor and was created 1st Baron Chelmsford. Thesiger purchased a commission in the Rifle Brigade and served at Halifax, Nova Scotia. In May 1855, he left for the Crimean War, in which he served firstly with his battalion, then as aide-de-camp to Lt-Gen. Edwin Markham. He served during the Indian Mutiny, ending as deputy adjutant-general to the forces in Bombay 1861-62. He was present at the 1868 expedition to Abyssinia, and was adjutant-general, India 1869-74.

Thesiger was promoted major-general in 1877 and appointed in 1878 to command the forces in South Africa with the local rank of lieutenant-general. In January 1879, Sir Henry Bartle Frere, a friend of Chelmsford, engineered a war against Cetshwayo, king of the Zulus, who at that time were an allied power by treaty with the British Crown. An expeditionary British military force under Chelmsford's command subsequently entered the Zulu kingdom uninvited, and was in consequence attacked on 22 January 1879 by a large Zulu army at Isandlwana, during which the Zulus overran and destroyed Chelmsford's separated forces. The engagement was an unexpected victory for the Zulus and one of the worst defeats of the British Army by native tribesmen. The Government issued orders for the hasty relief of Chelmsford of his command and for him to be replaced by Sir Garnet Wolseley. This could not be implemented until the arrival of Wolseley, and in the meantime Chelmsford ignored diplomatic peace overtures from King Cetshwayo and attacked the Zulus at Ulundi on 4 July 1879, this being the last major battle of the Anglo-Zulu War. Chelmsford attacked making full use of concentrated small arms fire from Gatling guns leading to the destruction of the Zulu force. He then ordered the royal kraal of Ulundi, the Zulu kingdom's capital, to be destroyed. Chelmsford was severely criticised by a subsequent enquiry launched by the British Army into the events that had led to the Isandlwana debacle and never served in the field again.

Far left: Frederic Augustus Thesiger, 2nd Baron Chelmsford, *c.* 1870.

Near left: Lord Chelmsford sketched by another officer at the Battle of Ulundi.

20   Sir Garnet Wolseley—the very model of a modern Major-General

Field Marshal Garnet Joseph Wolseley, 1st Viscount Wolseley (1833-1913), was born into an Anglo-Irish family in Dublin, eldest son of an army officer. At the age of 18 he was gazetted as an ensign in the 12th Foot, moving soon after to the 80th Foot with whom he served in the Second Anglo-Burmese War where he was severely wounded. After various promotions he fought at Crimea, losing an eye. Subsequent postings followed in the Far East, and in 1857 he was dispatched to Calcutta on account of the Indian Mutiny where he distinguished himself at the relief of Lucknow.

Left: Lieutenant-Colonel Garnet Wolseley VC, *c.* 1858, photograph by Felice Beato (1832-1909).

Right: Brevet-Colonel Garnet Wolseley, *c.* 1871.

In 1860 Wolseley accompanied the Anglo-French expedition to China and on his return home he published the *Narrative of the War with China in 1860*. He was given the substantive rank of major on 15 February 1861, and in November of that year he was one of the special service officers sent to Canada in connection with the Trent incident.

In 1862, shortly after the Battle of Antietam, Wolseley took leave from his military duties and went to investigate the American Civil War. He befriended Southern sympathizers in Maryland, who found him passage into Virginia with a blockade runner across the Potomac River. There he met with the Generals Robert E. Lee, James Longstreet and Stonewall Jackson. On his return to Canada he was actively employed in the defence of Canada from Fenian raids launched from the United States. In 1870 he successfully commanded the Red River Expedition to establish Canadian sovereignty over the Northwest Territories and Manitoba. After his success in this role, he returned home and was made a Knight Commander and a Companion of the Order of the Bath on 13 March 1871. He was then appointed assistant adjutant-general at the War Office in 1871 where he furthered the Cardwell schemes of army reform.

In 1873, Wolseley commanded the expedition to the Ashanti, and, having made all his arrangements at the Gold Coast before the arrival of the troops in January 1874, was able to complete the campaign in two months. This campaign made him a household name in Britain. At the Battle of Amoaful on 31 January of that year Wolseley's expedition faced and defeated the numerically superior Chief Amankwatia's army in a four-hour battle. For this he received the thanks of both houses of Parliament and a grant of £25,000, was promoted to brevet major-general for distinguished service in the field on 1 April 1874, and among other honours was made Knight Commander of the Order of the Bath. On his return home he was appointed inspector-general of auxiliary forces; however, in consequence of the indigenous unrest in Natal, he was sent to that colony as governor and general-commanding on 24 February 1875. Wolseley was promoted to the rank of major-general on 1 October 1877. He went as high commissioner to Cyprus on 12 July 1878, and in the following year to South Africa to supersede Lord Chelmsford in command of the forces in the Zulu War. Having reorganized the administration there and reduced the powerful king, Sekhukhune, to submission, he returned to London in May 1880 and as reward for his services he was advanced to Knight Grand Cross of the Order of the Bath on 19 June 1880. Finally as if to signify a meteoric rise in Imperial esteem he was appointed Quartermaster-General to the Forces on 1 July 1880.

On 1 September 1884, Wolseley was again called away from his duties as adjutant-general, to command the Nile Expedition for the relief of General Gordon and the besieged garrison at Khartoum, but the expedition arrived too late; Khartoum had been taken, and Gordon was dead.

Left: General Wolseley, *c.* 1885, the London Stereoscopic Company, Regent Street, London.

Right: George Grossmith as 'the very model of a modern Major-General' with exaggerated medals.

On 28 September 1885 he was created Viscount Wolseley, of Wolseley in the county of Stafford, and at the invitation of the queen, the Wolseley family moved from their home to the much grander Ranger's House in Greenwich in autumn 1888.

Wolseley continued at the War Office as adjutant-general to the forces until 1890, when he became commander-in-chief, Ireland. He was promoted to field marshal on 26 May 1894, and appointed by the government to succeed the duke of Cambridge as commander-in-chief of the Forces on 1 November 1895. This was the position to which his great experience in the field and his previous signal success at the War Office itself had fully entitled him, but it was increasingly irrelevant. Field Marshal Viscount Wolseley's powers in that office were, however, limited by a new Order in Council, and after holding the appointment for over five years, he handed over the command-in-chief to his fellow field marshal, Earl Roberts, on 3 January 1901. He had also suffered from a serious illness in 1897, from which he never fully recovered.

Left: Punch, 12 August 1882, 'Sir Garnet Wolseley—Short Service and Quick Returns'. Cartoon by Edward Linley Sambourne (1844-1910).

Below: An American view of the 'channel tunnel scare', from the magazine *Puck, c.* 1885. Cartoon by Friedrich Graetz (1840-1913). Wolseley was deeply opposed to Sir Edward Watkin's attempt to build a Channel Tunnel. He gave evidence to a parliamentary commission that the construction might be 'calamitous for England'.

21   Patience and the Aesthetic Movement

Patience, is a comic opera in two acts. It is clearly a satire on the aesthetic movement, and more broadly, on fads, superficiality, vanity, hypocrisy and pretentiousness; it also satirises romantic love, rural simplicity and military bluster. It was first performed at the Opera Comique, London, on 23 April 1881.

The aesthetic movement in Britain had its main influence from approximately 1860 to 1900. It aimed to escape the ugliness and materialism of the industrial age, by focusing instead on producing art that was beautiful rather than having a deeper meaning—'Art for Art's sake'. The artists and designers in this 'cult of beauty' crafted some of the most sophisticated and sensuously beautiful artworks of the Western tradition and in the process remade the domestic world of the British middle-classes. These new aesthetic artists included romantic bohemians such as Dante Gabriel Rossetti, William Morris and Edward Burne-Jones; maverick figures such as James McNeill Whistler and avant-garde architects and designers such as Edward William Godwin and Christopher Dresser; and the 'Olympians', the painters of grand classical subjects who belonged to the circle of Frederic Leighton and George Frederic Watts.

The Day Dream or, as it was initially intended to be named, *Monna Primavera*, 1880, by Dante Gabriel Rossetti, featuring his mistress, Jane Morris, wife of William Morris

Quite too Utterly Utter, songsheet cover, Alfred Concanen, about 1881. This was from a burlesque in the 'Oscar Polka Mazurka', published by F. W. Helmick, Cincinnati, Ohio, inspired by Oscar Wilde's US tour.

The figure of the aesthete, whose super-subtle sensibility and passionate response to works of art, emerged fully fledged in the 1870s. Considered to be tainted by unhealthy and possibly dangerous foreign ideas, the aesthete was treated with a considerable degree of suspicion by journalists and the general public. However, by the beginning of the 1880s the aesthete, with his self-proclaiming attachment to poetry, pictures and to the nuances of interior decoration—in short, the character so astutely adopted by Oscar Wilde—had become the popular butt of friendly satire. In both George Du Maurier's long-running series of sharply observed cartoons in *Punch* which had begun as early as 1876, the velvet-clad aesthetes were ridiculed for their 'stained-glass attitudes', overly precious speech, and enthusiasm for the curious appeal of pale lilies, sunflowers, peacock feathers, fragile blue-and-white china and Japanese fans.

Many *Punch* cartoons satirised æsthetes. Both *Patience* and *The Colonel* are mentioned here. A tiny, pennant-waving Gilbert peeks out of Sullivan's backpack at lower right. *The Colonel* was another work that satirised 'æsthetics'. According to F. C. Burnand's 1904 autobiography, Sullivan's friend Frederic Clay leaked to him the information that Gilbert and Sullivan were working on an 'æsthetic subject', and so Burnand raced to produce *The Colonel* before *Patience* opened. *The Colonel* beat *Patience* to the stage by several weeks, but *Patience* outran Burnand's play.

'Modjeska' was Polish actress Helena Modjeska (1840-1909), renowned for her Shakespearean and tragic roles who gained her fame in the USA. She spent the years 1879-82 in London to improve her English before returning to the stage in America. *Punch*, 7 May 1881.

Siegfried, Act II, drawing, by Aubrey Vincent Beardsley, *c.* 1892. Beardsley was a 'late entrant' to the aesthetic movement.

Aesthetic dress (*left and right*) contrasted with 'fashionable attire' (*centre*), entitled 'A Private View at the Royal Academy, 1881' by William Powell Frith (1819-1909).

22   Oscar Wilde

Oscar Fingal O'Flahertie Wills Wilde (1854-1900), was born in Dublin, the second son of Anglo-Irish Dublin intellectuals Sir William and Lady Jane Wilde. He was educated at Trinity College, Dublin and Magdalen College, Oxford. After university, Wilde moved to London into fashionable cultural and social circles.

Known for his biting wit, flamboyant dress and glittering conversation, Wilde became one of the best-known personalities of his day. He wrote one novel *The Picture of Dorian Gray* (1890), but was even better known for his plays which included *Lady Windermere's Fan*, *A Woman of No Importance*, and *An Ideal Husband*. At the time of his legal misfortunes he was at the height of his fame and success, with *The Importance of Being Earnest* (1895), being performed in London.

Richard D'Oyly Carte, was the booking manager for Oscar Wilde and employed him to publicise the 1881 Gilbert and Sullivan opera *Patience*—perfect casting since the opera was a satire on the aesthetic movement of which Wilde was an extreme example. The main character, 'Bunthorne', might even have been modelled on Wilde but Swinburne and Rossetti are also likely candidates. D'Oyly Carte sent Wilde on a lecture tour across the United States in order to illustrate what *Patience* was trying to satirize. Wilde and the operetta reaped invaluable publicity, prompting D'Oyly Carte to report: 'Inscrutable are the ways of the American public and absurd as it may appear, it seems that Oscar Wilde's advent here has caused a regular craze and given the business a fillip up'.

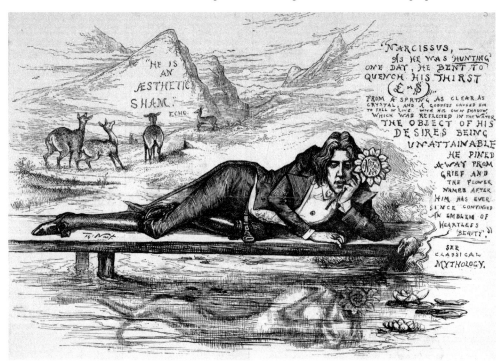

A cartoon, by American artist Thomas Nast (1840-1902), presumably inspired by the publication of six prose poems by Wilde in the magazine *The Fortnightly Review* of July 1894. One of them, 'The Disciples', is told from the point of view of the pool in which the Greek character Narcissus gazes lovingly at his own reflection. The background 'He is an aesthetic sham' is directly from *Patience*.

23   Richard D'Oyly Carte

Richard D'Oyly Carte (1844-1901) was born at his parents' house in London the eldest of six children. His father, Richard Carte (1808- 1891), was a flute-maker, flautist and composer, and his mother was Eliza, née Jones (1814-1885); the daughter of a Welsh clergyman. The name 'D'Oyly' was a forename, and not part of a surname.

After the completion of his education Carte joined his father's business. As the name Richard Carte was by now well known in, and beyond, the musical profession, Carte dropped the use of his own first name and styled himself 'R. D'Oyly Carte'. Carte went on to compose and publish a number of his own works. His musical compositions included an opera, *Dr. Ambrosias—His Secret*, first performed at St George's Opera House in 1868. However, he soon realised that his greater talent lay in management, and he launched a successful concert agency in Charing Cross. His many clients eventually included Charles Gounod, Jacques Offenbach, Adelina Patti, Mario, Clara Schumann, George Grossmith, James McNeill Whistler and Oscar Wilde among others. Gradually he began to drift towards light opera production. In 1875, during the run of one of these operas, Offenbach's *La Perichole* at the Royalty Theatre, Carte hit upon the idea that would launch the a great musical partnership. Attendance at the Royalty was down, and Carte suggested to Selina Delaro, for whom he was managing the theatre, that a new piece by W. S. Gilbert and Arthur Sullivan be added to the bill. The result was *Trial by Jury*, produced first on 25 March 1875. This was an immediate success, and was performed at many venues over the next two years.

Left: Richard D'Oyly Carte (1844-1901), *c.* 1876.

Right: Helen Couper Carte, née Lenoir (1858-1913), photographed in New York by Marc Gambier.

On one such tour (June to August 1876), Carte himself served as musical director of 'Mr. R. D'Oyly Carte's Opera Bouffe Company.' Full length works performed on this tour of Manchester, Liverpool, and Dublin were *La Perichole*, *La Fille de Madame Angot*, and *La Tibale*, with *Trial by Jury* and Carte's own one-act 'musical pastoral' *Happy Hampstead* serving as companion pieces.

Following this success Carte formed a syndicate to perform 'light opera of a legitimate kind', namely Gilbert and Sullivan operas, at the Opera Comique. The Comedy-Opera Company (Limited), as it was called, produced *The Sorcerer* and, in 1878, *H.M.S. Pinafore*. This opened to great enthusiasm but within days of the premiere London experienced an unusually strong and protracted heat wave, and business in the ill-ventilated Opera Comique was badly affected. Takings dropped to £40 a night, and Carte's directors in the Comedy Opera Company advocated cutting their losses and closing the show. After promotional efforts by Carte and Sullivan, who programmed some of the *Pinafore* music when he conducted a season of promenade concerts at Covent Garden, the opera became a hit. Carte convinced Gilbert and Sullivan that when their original agreement with the Comedy Opera Company expired in July 1879, a business partnership among the three of them would be to their advantage. Each put up £1,000 and formed a new partnership under the name 'Mr Richard D'Oyly Carte's Opera Company'. On 31 July 1879, the last day of their agreement with Carte, the directors of the Comedy Opera Company attempted to repossess the *Pinafore* set by force during a performance, causing a celebrated fracas. Carte's stagehands managed to ward off their backstage attackers and protect the scenery and props. The Comedy Opera Company opened a rival production of *H.M.S. Pinafore* in London, but it was not as popular as the D'Oyly Carte production and soon closed. Legal action over the ownership of the rights ended in victory for Carte, Gilbert and Sullivan. From 1 August 1879, the new company, later called the D'Oyly Carte Opera Company, became the sole authorised producer of the works of Gilbert and Sullivan.

Pinafore was followed in 1881 by *Patience* at the Opera Comique, and later that year *Patience* was transferred to Carte's new theatre on the Strand, the Savoy—the first theatre in London to be lighted entirely by electricity. Gilbert & Sullivan operas (both premieres and revivals) held the Savoy stage until 1891, when a rift between Carte and Gilbert known as the 'Carpet Quarrel' brought them to an abrupt end. Carte continued to produce comic opera at the Savoy, primarily works by Sullivan with other collaborators, but also filling the gaps with works by other composers. The break was eventually healed and Gilbert returned to the Savoy again in 1893 (with *Utopia Limited*) and 1896 (with *The Grand Duke*).

In 1891, Carte produced Sullivan's 'grand opera' *Ivanhoe* to launch his new Royal English Opera House in Cambridge Circus. It was Carte's idea to establish serious British opera there as a regular institution, but this never came to pass. When *Ivanhoe* closed after a successful run there was no British opera to succeed it. Andre Messager's *La Basoche* was brought in to fill the gap, and then the theatre was let to Madame Sarah Bernhardt for a season. Carte finally abandoned the project and sold the theatre to a syndicate. It was then converted into a music hall.

Carte also became a famous hotelier. The Savoy Hotel, designed by the architect Thomas Edward Collcutt, opened in 1889. Financed by profits from *The Mikado*, it was the first hotel lit by electric lights and the first with electric lifts. In the 1890s, under its famous manager, César Ritz, and chef Auguste Escoffier, it became a well-known luxury hotel and would generate more income and contribute more to the D'Oyly Carte fortunes than any other enterprise, including the opera companies. Carte later acquired and refurbished Claridge's (1893), The Grand Hotel in Rome (1896), Simpson's-in-the-Strand (1898) and The Berkeley (1900).

Above: The Savoy Hotel and Restaurant *c.* 1895.

Below: The Savoy Hotel, viewed from the Thames, *c.* 1891, taken from contemporary publicity material.

Carte was married twice. His first wife was Blanche Julia Prowse (1853-1885). As a teenager, she had participated in amateur theatricals with Carte. They married in 1870 and had two sons, Lucas (1872-1907) and Rupert (1876-1948). Blanche died of pneumonia in 1885, and in 1888, Carte married his assistant, Helen Lenoir. Their wedding took place in the Savoy Chapel, with Arthur Sullivan as the best man.

Sullivan's affiliation with the Cartes never wavered. He was composing for the Savoy right up until his death in 1900. Carte managed the D'Oyly Carte Opera Company for the rest of his life, though during his last years he had considerable support from his second wife and long-time assistant, Helen. As Helen Couper Lenoir, she had managed his operations in America in the early 1880s. After Carte's death, she managed the D'Oyly Carte Opera Company until her own passing in 1913.

Left: George Grossmith comforts Richard D'Oyly Carte after failure of *The Grand Duke*, 'Good times will come again, D'Oyly my boy!' A cartoon by Alfred Bryan (1852-1899).

Right: Richard D'Oyly Carte by 'Spy', Leslie Ward, published in *Vanity Fair*, 1 January, 1891.

24   *George Grossmith as Reginald Bunthorne*

Grossmith was famous as Reginald Bunthorne, a character from *Patience* whom he performed with relish and outstanding success. Grossmith said of his work as an entertainer: 'To clown properly is a very difficult art, and I am never so happy as when I am making people laugh. I am unfeignedly proud of my profession, on and off the stage. … On the stage I play the fool of others' creation, and at the piano I play the simple fool of my own.'

Above, left and right, and below left: George Grossmith as Reginald Bunthorne in *Patience*.

Below right: A studio photograph by Herbert Rose Barraud *c.* 1885.

25   Lord Randolph Churchill

Lord Randolph Henry Spencer-Churchill (1849-1895) was a Tory radical and coined the term 'Tory democracy'. He inspired a generation of party managers, created the National Union of the Conservative Party, and broke new ground in modern budgetary presentations, attracting admiration and criticism from across the political spectrum. His most acerbic critics resided in his own party among his closest friends; but his disloyalty to Lord Salisbury was the beginning of the end of what should have been a glittering career. His elder son, Winston, wrote a biography of him in 1906. Churchill was chancellor of the Exchequer in the marquess of Salisbury's administration for the brief period of August to December 1886.

The so-called Tory Democrat Lord Randolph Churchill could not resist labelling W. H. Smith (and another middle-class man Richard Cross) as not only 'bourgeois placemen' but also the veritable 'Marshall and Snelgrove' of the Conservative party. A remark in distinctly Gilbertian mode, and he was another of the type of minister to be lampooned. (Marshall & Snelgrove was a department store on the north side of Oxford Street, London).

LORD RANDOLPH CHURCHILL, M.P.

THERE IS A MIDGE AT WESTMINSTER,
A GNATTY LITTLE THING,
IT BITES AT NIGHT
THIS MIGHTY MITE,
BUT NO ONE FEELS ITS STING,
ITS NOISE PERSISTENT, SHRILL,—SO SOME
SAY THERE'S NO STING, BUT 'TIS ALL "HUM."

Left: Lord Randolph Churchill, a studio photograph, 1883.

Right: 1881 *Punch* cartoon by Edward Linley Sambourne of Lord Randolph Churchill, MP, as a 'midge with no sting in Parliament'.

The Japanese Village in Knightsbridge, London, was an exhibition which took place from January 1885 until June 1887. The setting was built to resemble a traditional Japanese village. The exhibition was a commercial venture organised by Tannaker Buhicrosan, who had been organising travelling Japanese exhibitions in Britain for several years beforehand. As a result of the opening up of Japan to trade with Britain in the 1850s, an English craze for all things Japanese had built through the 1860s and 1870s, fed by the British perception of Japan as a medieval culture. This resonated particularly with devotees of the aesthetic movement of the late nineteenth century and made the exhibition very popular, with over one million visitors in total.

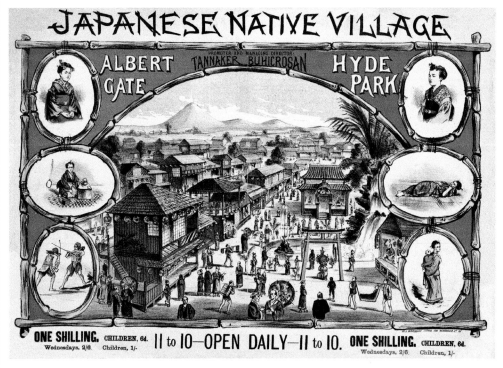

A contemporary poster for the Japanese Native Village.

The exhibition was built to resemble a traditional Japanese village, completely contained within Humphreys' Hall (which was south of Knightsbridge and east of what is now Trevor Street). It employed around 100 Japanese men and women, and included segregated sleeping accommodation. According to advertisements placed in *The Illustrated London News*:

> Skilled Japanese artisans and workers (male and female) will illustrate the manners, customs, and art-industries of their country, attired in their national and picturesque costumes. Magnificently decorated and illuminated Buddhist temple. Five o'clock tea in the Japanese tea-house. Japanese Musical and other Entertainments. Every-day Life as in Japan.

While Gilbert and Sullivan were writing their opera *The Mikado* (1885), W. S. Gilbert visited the exhibition and engaged Japanese people from the village to teach his cast aspects of Japanese behaviour.

Gilbert had already commented on this fascination a few years earlier in his spoof of Oscar Wilde in *Patience* (1882). When the sham aesthete 'Bunthorne' has a moment alone, he sings the following confession:

> I do not long for all one sees
> That's Japanese.
> I am not fond of uttering platitudes
> In stained glass attitudes.
> In short, my mediaevalism's affectation,
> Born of a morbid love of admiration!

The exhibition was not the genesis of *The Mikado*—because this opened at the Savoy a mere two months after the opening of the exhibition—but the visual experience did allow Gilbert to add touches of reality to his work.

In May 1885, the hall burnt down overnight and one of the Japanese employees was killed in the blaze. However Buhicrosan immediately announced that the hall and the exhibit would be rebuilt as quickly as possible. As it happened the exhibit employees were already committed to visit Berlin and appear at the 1885 International Hygiene Exhibition in Berlin. They proceeded to fulfil the engagement. Meanwhile, the hall and the village exhibit were both reconstructed and the exhibition re-opened to the public in December 1885.

The Japanese Village Exhibition in London, an engraving by Arthur Hopkins published in *The Graphic*, 4 January 1890.

The Two Very Fanny Japs at the Savoy.

Above left: The Japanese village, a photograph taken personally by W. S. Gilbert.

Above right: Punch, 28 March 1885.

Below: Punch, 24 January 1885.

AN ENGLISH VILLAGE FROM A JAPANESE POINT OF VIEW.

27 The Lord Chamberlain

The Lord Chamberlain is the most senior officer of the Royal Household, supervising the departments which support and provide advice to the sovereign, also acting as the main channel of communication between the sovereign and the House of Lords. In 1737, Sir Robert Walpole officially introduced statutory censorship with the Licensing Act of 1737 by appointing the Lord Chamberlain to act as the theatrical censor. In 1909, a Joint Select Committee on Stage Plays (Censorship) was established and recommended that the Lord Chamberlain should continue to act as censor but that it could be lawful to perform plays without a licence from the Lord Chamberlain. However, King Edward VII refused to accept these recommendations.

In the 1960s the debate to abolish theatre censorship rose again as a new generation of young play-wrights came on the scene, but since many were refused a licence by the Lord Chamberlain, they could not transfer to the West End. In the case of John Osborne's play *A Patriot for Me*, the Lord Chamberlain at the time, Lord Cobbold, was irritated that the play was so widely publicised even though he had banned it and therefore pursued legal action. In the end, the play was allowed to continue as it was. At this point, several widely regarded authors had all been censored by the Lord Chamberlain at one time or another, including playwrights Henrik Ibsen and George Bernard Shaw. Another Joint Select Committee was founded to further debate on the issue and present a solution. After much debate, the Theatres Act 1968 was finally passed; it officially abolished the censorship of the stage and repealed the Lord Chamberlain's power to refuse a licence to a play of any kind. The first London performance of the musical *Hair* was actually delayed until the Act was passed after a licence had been refused.

The Lord Chamberlain in 1907 was Charles Robert Spencer, 6th Earl Spencer (1857-1922). He served as Vice-Chamberlain of the Household from 1892 to 1895. He was Lord Chamberlain from 1905 to 1912 in the Liberal administrations headed by Campbell-Bannerman and Asquith, and it was Spencer who forbad all stage presentations of *The Mikado*. In 1910, he succeeded his half-brother in the earldom of Spencer.

Charles Robert Spencer, 6th Earl Spencer, *c.* 1900.

Gilbert built the Garrick Theatre in 1889 and he and Lucy moved to Grim's Dyke in Harrow in 1890. After casting Nancy McIntosh in *Utopia, Limited*, he and his wife developed an affection for her, and she eventually gained the status of an unofficially adopted daughter, moving to Grim's Dyke to live with them. She continued living there, even after Gilbert died, until Lady Gilbert's death in 1936.

Following the 'Carpet Affair' there were many failed attempts at reconciliation. Eventually Tom Chappell, the music publisher responsible for printing the Gilbert and Sullivan operas, stepped in to mediate between two of his most profitable artists, and within two weeks had succeeded. Two more operas resulted: *Utopia, Limited* (1893) and *The Grand Duke* (1896). Gilbert also offered a third libretto to Sullivan, but Gilbert's insistence on casting Nancy McIntosh, led to Sullivan's refusal. Sullivan continued to compose comic opera with other librettists but died four years later.

William Schwenck Gilbert, 1886 by Frank Holl (1845-1888). *National Portrait Gallery*

Although Gilbert announced a retirement from the theatre after the short run of *The Grand Duke* (1896) and the poor reception of his 1897 play *The Fortune Hunter*, he produced at least three more plays over the last dozen years of his life, including an unsuccessful opera, *Fallen Fairies* (1909), with Edward German. His last play, *The Hooligan*, produced just four months before his death, is a study of a young condemned thug in a prison cell. Gilbert shows sympathy for his protagonist, the son of a thief who, brought up among thieves, kills his girlfriend. As in some earlier work, the playwright displays 'his conviction that nurture rather than nature often accounted for criminal behaviour'. The grim and powerful piece became one of Gilbert's most successful serious dramas, and experts conclude that, in those last months of Gilbert's life, he was developing a new style, a 'mixture of irony, of social theme, and of grubby realism'.

Gilbert was knighted on 15 July 1907 in recognition of his contributions to drama, the first British writer ever to receive a knighthood for his plays alone. On 29 May 1911, Gilbert was about to give a swimming lesson to two young women, Winifred Isabel Emery (1890-1972), and 17-year-old Ruby Preece in the lake of his home, Grim's Dyke, when Preece got into difficulties and called for help. Gilbert dived in to save her but suffered a heart attack in the middle of the lake and died at the age of 74. Gilbert's memorial on the south wall of the Thames Embankment in London reads: 'His Foe was Folly, and his Weapon Wit'.

PUNCH'S FANCY PORTRAITS.—No. 43.

MR. W. S. GILBERT.

BUT IN SPITE OF SOME TEMPTATIONS
TO TRANSLATIONS AND SENSATIONS,
HE REMAINS——
A SORCERER YOUNG MAN,
A *PINAFORE PIRATES* MAN,
A BRILLIANT WHAT I CALL QUITE IDI-YACHT-ICAL
BALLADY BAB YOUNG MAN.

Left: W. S. Gilbert with a caption reading 'Patience', *Vanity Fair*, 21 May 1881; by 'Spy', Leslie Ward (1851-1922).

Right: *Punch*, 6 August 1881, cartoon by Edward Linley Sambourne (1844-1910).

Gilbert was known for being prickly on occasions. Aware of this general impression, he claimed that 'If you give me your attention', the misanthrope's song from *Princess Ida*, was a satiric self-reference, saying: 'I thought it my duty to live up to my reputation'. However, many people have defended him, often citing his generosity. Actress May Fortescue recalled, 'His kindness was extraordinary. On wet nights and when rehearsals were late and the last buses were gone, he would pay the cab-fares of the girls whether they were pretty or not, instead of letting them trudge home on foot ... He was just as large-hearted when he was poor as when he was rich and successful. For money as money he cared less than nothing. Gilbert was no plaster saint, but he was an ideal friend'. The journalist Frank M. Boyd wrote:

I fancy that seldom was a man more generally given credit for a personality quite other than his own, than was the case with Sir W. S. Gilbert ... Till one actually came to know the man, one shared the opinion held by so many, that he was a gruff, disagreeable person; but nothing could be less true of the really great humorist. He had rather a severe appearance ... and like many other clever people, he had precious little use for fools of either sex, but he was at heart as kindly and lovable a man as you could wish to meet.

Jessie Bond wrote that Gilbert 'was quick-tempered, often unreasonable, and he could not bear to be thwarted, but how anyone could call him unamiable I cannot understand.' George Grossmith wrote to *The Daily Telegraph* that, although Gilbert had been described as an autocrat at rehearsals:

… That was really only his manner when he was playing the part of stage director at rehearsals. As a matter of fact, he was a generous, kind true gentleman, and I use the word in the purest and original sense.

Grossmith later added:

During my dangerous illness, Mr Gilbert never failed a day to come up and enquire after me ... and kept me in roars of laughter the whole time ... But to see Gilbert at his best, is to see him at one of his juvenile parties. Though he has no children of his own, he loves them, and there is nothing he would not do to please them. I was never so astonished as when on one occasion he put off some of his own friends to come with Mrs Gilbert to a juvenile party at my own house.

Sir W. S. Gilbert in his later years.

According to one London society lady:

[Gilbert]'s wit was innate, and his rapier-like retorts slipped out with instantaneous ease. His mind was naturally fastidious and clean; he never asserted himself, never tried to make an effect. He was great-hearted and most understanding, with an underlying poetry of fancy that made him the most delicious companion. They spoke of his quick temper, but that was entirely free from malice or guile. He was soft-hearted as a babe, but there was nothing of the hypocrite about him. What he thought he said on the instant, and though by people of sensitive vanity this might on occasion be resented, to a sensitiveness of a finer kind it was an added link, binding one to a faithful, valued friend.

As for his differences with Arthur Sullivan, these should also be look at in context with his personality. In 1904, Gilbert would write, '... Savoy opera was snuffed out by the deplorable death of my distinguished collaborator, Sir Arthur Sullivan. When that event occurred, I saw no one with whom I felt that I could work with satisfaction and success, and so I discontinued to write libretti.'

Gilbert once relayed to his friend, author Henry Rowland-Brown, that after his death, he wished to be buried in the gardens at Grim's Dyke—as he loved them so much, but it was not to be. After his death from a heart attack in the lake at Grim's Dyke he was cremated at Golders Green and his ashes buried at the churchyard of St John's Church, Stanmore.

'The Ironmaster', a cartoon from 1885 by Alfred Bryan (1852-99) that appeared in *The Ent'racte Annual* for that year. W. S. Gilbert is depicted in a suit of armour, wielding a mallet labelled 'discipline' and towering over the diminutive figure of Richard D'Oyly Carte. When this was published, *The Ironmaster*, a play by Sir Arthur Wing Pinero (1855-1934), first performed 17 April 1884, had recently finished a successful run of 200 performances at the St James's Theatre, so this cartoon was a reference to a different type of 'iron master' at the Savoy Theatre.

The Ironmaster at the Savoy.

Sullivan's first opera, *The Sapphire Necklace* (1863-64), is now lost, except for the overture and two songs. His first surviving opera, *Cox and Box* (1866), was produced at the Gallery of Illustration, where it ran for 264 performances. Gilbert, writing in *Fun* magazine, pronounced the score superior to Burnand's libretto. Sullivan and Burnand were soon commissioned for a two-act opera, *The Contrabandista*, (1867); but it did not do as well.

Sullivan first met Gilbert at a rehearsal for a second run of Gilbert's *Ages Ago* at the Gallery of Illustration, probably in July 1870, but nothing came of this encounter. In 1871 Sullivan wrote the music to the hymn *Onward, Christian Soldiers*, the words of which had been penned by Sabine Baring-Gould. At the end of 1871 John Hollingshead, proprietor of London's Gaiety Theatre, commissioned Sullivan to work with Gilbert to create the burlesque-style comic opera *Thespis*. Gilbert and Sullivan then went their separate ways until they collaborated on three parlour ballads in late 1874 and early 1875.

Left: Arthur Seymour Sullivan with a caption reading 'English Music', *Vanity Fair*, 14 March 1874; by 'Ape', Carlo Pellegrini (1839-1889).

Right: 'Don't find composing comic opera as easy as you thought, do you, Mackenzie?' Cartoon by Alfred Bryan, alluding to the failure of *His Majesty* (1897), after Alexander Mackenzie (1847-1935) had criticised Sullivan for 'wasting his talents' on comic opera. It was with a libretto by F. C. Burnand, lyrics by R. C. Lehmann, additional lyrics by Adrian Ross and music by Mackenzie. The work premiered at the Savoy Theatre on 20 February 1897, running for only 61 performances until 24 April 1897, despite a strong cast including George Grossmith.

In 1875, Richard D'Oyly Carte, needed a piece to fill out a bill with Offenbach's *La Périchole*. Carte had conducted Sullivan's *Cox and Box*. Remembering that Gilbert had suggested a libretto to him, Carte engaged Sullivan to set it, and the result was the one-act comic opera *Trial by Jury*. Starring Sullivan's brother Fred as the 'Learned Judge', it became a hit, earning praise from the critics and playing for 300 performances. *The Daily Telegraph* commented that the piece illustrated the composer's 'great capacity for dramatic writing of the lighter class', and other reviews emphasised the felicitous combination of Gilbert's words and Sullivan's music. A few months later, another Sullivan one-act comic opera opened: *The Zoo*, with a libretto by B. C. Stephenson. It was less successful than *Trial*, and for the next 15 years Sullivan's sole operatic collaborator was Gilbert.

Sullivan's next collaboration with Gilbert, *The Sorcerer* (1877), ran for 178 performances, but *H.M.S. Pinafore* (1878), turned Gilbert and Sullivan into an international phenomenon. Pinafore ran for 571 performances in London, then the second-longest theatrical run in history, and more than 150 unauthorised productions were quickly mounted in America alone. Pinafore was followed by *The Pirates of Penzance* in 1879, which opened in New York (to beat the copyright pirates at their own game) and then ran in London for 363 performances.

In February 1883, he and Gilbert signed a five-year agreement with Carte, and on 22 May of the same year he was knighted by Queen Victoria for his 'services ... rendered to the promotion of the art of music'.

Left: Portrait of Sir Arthur Sullivan, *c.* 1880, by John Everett Millais (1829-1896). *National Portrait Gallery*

Right: Sir Arthur Seymour Sullivan, a studio photograph, *c.* 1885, probably by Count Stanisław Julian Ostroróg (1834-1890).

For almost two years Gilbert and Sullivan were at impasse, the latter continually rejecting Gilbert's ideas. This was finally resolved in May 1884 when Gilbert proposed a plot that did not depend on any supernatural device. The result was their most successful work, *The Mikado* (1885), running for 672 performances.

Sullivan wished to produce serious works with Gilbert; he had collaborated with no other librettist since 1875. Gilbert finally proposed a comparatively serious opera, to which Sullivan agreed, and *The Yeomen of the Guard* was the result, but Gilbert did not wish to continue, feeling that the reaction had 'not been so convincing as to warrant us in assuming that the public want something more earnest still'. He proposed instead that Sullivan should go ahead with his plan to write a grand opera, but should continue also to compose comic works for the Savoy. Sullivan was not immediately persuaded. He replied, 'I have lost the liking for writing comic opera, and entertain very grave doubts as to my power of doing it'. Nevertheless, Sullivan soon suggested to Gilbert that he revive an old idea for an opera set in colourful Venice. *The Gondoliers* (1889) was a piece described by Gervase Hughes as a pinnacle of Sullivan's achievement. It was the last great Gilbert and Sullivan success. The relationship between Gilbert and Sullivan then suffered its most serious breach in April 1890, in the 'Carpet Affair'.

 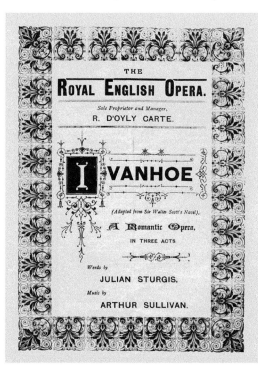

Left: Mary Frances 'Fanny' Ronalds (1839-1916) was an American socialite and amateur singer who is best known for her long affair with Arthur Sullivan and for her musical salons.

Right: The front cover of original theatre programme for Richard D'Oyly Carte's 1891 production of *Ivanhoe*.

Sullivan's only grand opera, *Ivanhoe*, based on Walter Scott's novel, opened at Carte's new Royal English Opera House on 31 January 1891. Sullivan completed the score too late to meet Carte's planned production date, and costs mounted; Sullivan was required to pay Carte a contractual penalty of £3,000 for his delay. The production lasted for 155 consecutive performances, an unprecedented run for a grand opera, and earned good notices for its music. Afterwards, Carte was unable to fill the new opera house with other opera productions and sold the theatre. Despite the initial success of *Ivanhoe*, it soon passed into obscurity.

Sullivan returned to comic opera, but because of the fracture with Gilbert, he and Carte sought other collaborators. Sullivan's next piece was *Haddon Hall* (1892), with a libretto by Sydney Grundy. It ran for 204 performances, and was popular with amateur theatre groups, up to the 1920s, but it has been produced only sporadically since then.

With the aid of an intermediary, Sullivan's music publisher Tom Chappell, the three partners were reunited in 1892 and two more operas were performed; *Utopia, Limited* (1893), and *The Grand Duke* (1896). This latter piece failed, and Sullivan never worked with Gilbert again, although their operas continued to be revived with success at the Savoy.

Sullivan never married, but had several love affairs. The first was with Rachel Scott Russell, and by 1865 the affair was in full bloom. Rachel's parents did not approve of a possible union with a young composer of uncertain financial prospects, but the two continued to see each other covertly. At some point in 1868 Sullivan started a simultaneous (and secret) affair with Rachel's sister Louise. Both relationships ended by early 1869. Sullivan's longest love affair was with the American socialite Fanny Ronalds. He met her in Paris around 1867, and the affair began in earnest soon after she moved to London in 1871. Sullivan called her 'the best amateur singer in London'. Fanny was separated from her husband, but they never divorced. Sullivan had a roving eye, and his diary records the occasional quarrels when Fanny discovered his other liaisons, but he always returned to her. Around 1889 or 1890 the sexual relationship evidently ended, but she remained a constant companion for the remainder of his life. In 1896 the 54-year-old Sullivan proposed marriage to the 22-year-old Violet Beddington, but she refused him.

Sullivan loved to spend time in France, in Paris and at the Riviera, where the casinos enabled him to indulge his passion for gambling. He enjoyed hosting private dinners and entertainments at his home, often featuring famous singers and well-known actors. Sullivan also enjoyed playing tennis; according to George Grossmith, 'I have seen some bad lawn-tennis players in my time, but I never saw anyone so bad as Arthur Sullivan'.

Sullivan's health was never robust—he composed the bright and cheerful music of *Pinafore* while suffering from excruciating pain from a kidney stone. From his thirties his kidney disease often obliged him to conduct sitting down. He died of heart failure, following an attack of bronchitis, at his flat in London on 22 November 1900.

30   The Carpet Affair

In April 1890, during the run of *The Gondoliers*, Gilbert discovered that maintenance expenses for the theatre, including a new £500 carpet for the front lobby of the theatre, were charged to the partnership instead of being borne by Carte. Although the cost was not that significant in the greater scheme of things, Gilbert felt that it was a moral issue involving Carte's integrity, and he could not look past it.

Gilbert was said by many people to be a kind and generous man, but he was known to have had an impetuous and volatile temperament at times. He may have harboured suspicions about Carte during the lavish building and fitting out of the Savoy Hotel and there is the distinct possibility of jealousy at the closeness between Carte and Sullivan—the latter had been the former's best man at Carte's marriage two years earlier.

On 22 April 1890, Gilbert wrote to Sullivan:

> I have had a difficulty with Carte.
>
> I was appalled to learn from him that the preliminary expenses of the Gondoliers amounted to the stupendous sum of £4,500!!! This seemed so utterly unaccountable that I asked to see the details and last night I received a resumé of them.… But the most surprising item was £500 for new carpets for the front of the house!

According to the 1883 contract, 'all expenses and charges of producing the ... operas and all the performances of the same, including ... repairs incidental to the performance', were to be deducted from the profits of the operas, the remainder then being distributed equally between Gilbert, Sullivan and Carte. Gilbert contended that new carpets for the front of the house—which would last far longer than the production in hand—could not be called 'repairs incidental to the performance'. In the same letter, Gilbert describes the row he had with Carte over these expenses. The carpet was only one of the items which Gilbert took exception to. Sullivan did not really wish to get involved, but agreed to look into the matter. Gilbert wanted a new contract with Carte which would be more transparent, but Sullivan seemed anxious to delay this, saying that the existing dispute over expenses should be settled first. Sullivan was certainly anxious to keep on good terms with Carte, for whom he was about to write his Grand Opera *Ivanhoe*. But he was also trying to avoid falling out with Gilbert.

It seems probable that Carte was taking advantage, but Gilbert also exaggerated, and Carte himself insisted that Gilbert had mistaken the cost of the carpet: it was not £500, but only £140.

Gilbert was not slow to realise Sullivan's lack of support. On 5 May 1890 he wrote to Sullivan: 'The time for putting an end to our collaboration has at last arrived'. Gilbert then took legal action. Carte sent him £2,000, but Gilbert calculated his share to be at least £3,000, and on his solicitor's advice applied for a receiver to deal with the Gondoliers accounts. After two adjournments, the case came before the court on 3 September 1890, and was settled the same day. Carte was to pay Gilbert a further £1,000, but Gilbert's application for a receiver was refused. When the case was over, Gilbert, feeling that his attitude had been vindicated in the court of law, tried to organise a reconciliation with Carte and Sullivan. The others were not feeling as amicable; Richard D'Oyly Carte refused to meet him, though his wife Helen agreed to do so. As for Sullivan, he wanted to be reconciled to Gilbert, but Gilbert would only consent to this if Sullivan retracted an affidavit which he had made in the court case, which had effectively accused Gilbert of perjury, but not surprisingly Sullivan refused to do so.

Eventually after two years had passed some form of reconciliation *was* reached. They produced *Utopia, Limited* in 1893 and *The Grand Duke* in 1896, but neither of these even approached the best of the Savoy series. Gilbert had lost much of his youthful exuberance and Sullivan had lost his enthusiasm for setting Gilbert's words.

Left: Mr W. S. Gilbert: 'Well D'Oyly, and when do you think you will want me again?' A cartoon from *The Entr'acte Annual*, 1891, by Alfred Bryan (1852-1899). Arthur Sullivan's *Ivanhoe* was a success, but D'Oyly Carte had nothing to go on after it, and so the opera house had to close, and would eventually fail.

Right: The Entr'acte, Loq.: 'Glad to see you together, gentlemen. You'll find this more profitable than pulling different ways.' A cartoon from *Entr'acte Annual*, 1893, by Alfred Bryan (1852-1899). Richard D'Oyly Carte, W. S. Gilbert, and Arthur Sullivan together again for *Utopia, Limited*, after the carpet quarrel.

31 Darwinism

Darwinism gained general scientific acceptance following the publication of *On the Origin of Species* in 1859 by Charles Darwin (1809-1882). The biologist Thomas Henry Huxley coined the term 'Darwinism' in April 1860.

Darwin's contemporaries eventually came to accept the transmutation of species based upon fossil evidence, and the X Club was formed to defend evolution against the church and wealthy amateurs. Protestantism, especially in America, broke out in 'acrid polemics' and argument about evolution from 1860 to the 1870s. In Britain, while publication of *The Descent of Man* by Darwin in 1871 reinvigorated debate from the previous decade, Sir Henry Chadwick notes a steady acceptance of evolution 'among more educated Christians' between 1860 and 1885. As a result, evolutionary theory was 'both permissible and respectable' by 1876. Notwithstanding this gradual acceptance, debate was lively, especially among the less well educated classes. W. S. Gilbert capitalises on this in his libretto for *Princess Ida*:

> … A Lady fair, of lineage high,
> Was loved by an Ape, in the days gone by.
> The Maid was radiant as the sun,
> The Ape was a most unsightly one …
> With a view to rise in the social scale,
> He shaved his bristles and he docked his tail …
> He bought white ties, and he bought dress suits,
> He crammed his feet into bright tight boots —
> And to start in life on a brand-new plan,
> He christened himself Darwinian Man!

Left: Charles Darwin, photographed by Julia Margaret Cameron, 1868.

Right: 'A Venerable Orang-outang', a caricature of Charles Darwin as an ape published in *The Hornet*, a satirical magazine, 22 March 1871.

Gallery of the D'Oyly Carte Opera Company
Some of principal performers from the late 1870s to the mid-1890s

Left: George Grossmith as Major-General Stanley in the original London production of *The Pirates of Penzance*.

Right: Rutland Barrington (1853-1922), born as George Rutland Fleet, a baritone in the Doyly Carte Opera Company, as Earl of Mountararat in *Iolanthe*.

Left: Durward Lely (1852-1944), born as James Durward Lyall, a principal tenor in the Doyly Carte Opera Company, as Nanki-Poo in *The Mikado*, 1885.

Right: Richard [Barker Cobb] Temple (1846-1912), was a bass-baritone in the Doyly Carte Opera Company, as The Pirate King in *The Pirates of Penzance*, 1880.

Left: Charles Courtice Pounds (1861-1927), better known by the stage name Courtice Pounds, was a tenor in the D'Oyly Carte Opera Company. A studio photograph by Sarony, 87 Union Square, New York.

Right: Jessie [Charlotte] Bond (1853-1942), was a mezzo-soprano in the D'Oyly Carte Opera Company. A studio photograph by Herbert Rose Barraud, Oxford Street, London.

Left: Sybil Grey (1860-1939), born Ellen Sophia Taylor, was a singer and actress best known for creating a series of minor (but important) roles in the D'Oyly Carte Opera Company, as Sacharissa in *Princess Ida* (1884). A studio photograph by Elliott and Fry, Baker Street, London.

Right: Frank Wyatt (1852-1926), is best remembered for his roles with the D'Oyly Carte Opera Company from 1889 to 1891, and in particular for creating the role of the duke of Plaza-Toro in *The Gondoliers*.

Left: George Edwardes (1855-1915), born Edwards, moved to London to work for Carte at the Opera Comique in the late 1870s. In 1885 he was hired to succeed John Hollingshead as manager at the Gaiety Theatre. He was later Carte's managing director of the Savoy Hotel. A studio photograph by Ellis & Walery.

Right: Julia Gwynne (1856-1934), born Julia Lavinia Putney, was a singer and actress best remembered for her performances with the D'Oyly Carte Opera Company from 1879 to 1883. She married George Edwardes, a manager for Richard D'Oyly Carte at the Opera Comique and the Gaiety Theatre. A studio photograph by Elliott and Fry, Baker Street, London.

Left: Rosina Brandram (1845-1907), born Rosina Moult, joined the D'Oyly Carte Opera Company in 1877 in the chorus. She was primarily known for creating many of the contralto roles with the Company. A studio photograph by Ellis & Walery, London.

Right: John Clark (1841-1906), better known as Signor Brocolini, was an Irish-born American singer and actor remembered for creating the role of the Pirate King in the original New York City production of *The Pirates of Penzance*, in 1879–80. A studio photograph by Mora, New York. *Harvard Theatre Collection, Houghton Library*

Left: Fred Billington (1854-1917), was best known for his baritone roles with the D'Oyly Carte Opera Company. He joined the Company begun in 1879 and created the role of the Sergeant of Police in the one-off performance of *The Pirates of Penzance* given in December 1879 in Paignton (the day prior to the New York premiere) to establish Gilbert's and Sullivan's British copyright. *Harvard Theatre Collection, Houghton Library*

Right: Louisa Emma Amelia 'Louie' Pounds (1872-1970), was known for her performances in in mezzo-soprano roles with the D'Oyly Carte Opera Company. She joined the Company in 1899. Her older brother Courtice was a principal tenor with the Company in the 1880s and 1890s.

Left: Charles H. [Herbert] Workman (1872-1923), was a singer and actor best known as a successor to George Grossmith in the comic baritone roles. He joined the D'Oyly Carte Opera Company in 1894. Workman created the small part of Ben Hashbaz in *The Grand Duke* (1896).

Right: Geraldine Ulmar (1862-1932), was an American singer and actress, best known for her performances in soprano roles of the D'Oyly Carte Opera Company. In 1879, she made her professional debut in the role of Josephine in *H.M.S. Pinafore*, aboard a ship in a lake in Boston's Oakland Garden. A studio photograph by Alfred Ellis, 20 Upper Baker Street, London.

Left: Courtice Pounds as Richard Dauntless in *Ruddigore*. A studio photograph by Falk, of 949 Broadway, New York.

Right: Richard Temple, Frank Thornton and Durward Lely in *Patience*. A studio photograph by Elliott and Fry, Baker Street, London.

Left: Sybil Grey as Peep-Bo, Leonora Braham as Yum-Yum and Jessie Bond as Pitti-Sing—the three sisters, wards of Ko-Ko from *The Mikado*. A studio photograph by Herbert Rose Barraud, 1885.

Right: Sybil Grey as Flete and Julia Gwynne as Leila in *Iolanthe*.

Left: Richard Temple as Strephon and Leonora Braham as Phyllis, in *Iolanthe*, 1882.

Right: George Grossmith as The Lord Chancellor in *Iolanthe*. A studio photograph by Elliott and Fry, Baker Street, London.

Left: Rutland Barrington and Courtice Pounds as Giuseppe and Marco in *The Gondoliers*.

Right: Rosina Brandram as Lady Jane in *Patience*, *c*. 1900. A studio photograph by Alfred Ellis & Walery, London. *Harvard Theatre Collection, Houghton Library*

Gallery of the Gilbert and Sullivan Operas

Thespis Or, The Gods Grown Old
(26 December 1871, 63 performances)

Clement Scott, writing in *The Daily Telegraph*, had a mostly favourable reaction:

> … Certain it is, however, that the greeting which awaited *Thespis, or The Gods Grown Old*, was not so cordial as might have been expected. The story, written by Mr. W. S. Gilbert in his liveliest manner, is so original, and the music contributed by Mr. Arthur Sullivan so pretty and fascinating, that we are inclined to be disappointed when we find the applause fitful, the laughter scarcely spontaneous, and the curtain falling not without sounds of disapprobation. Such a fate as this was certainly not deserved, and the verdict of last evening cannot be taken as final.

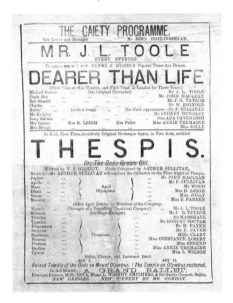

Above left: Opening night programme, *Thespis*, The Gaiety Theatre, 26 December 1871. Arthur Sullivan conducting, with his brother Frederic cast in the character of Apollo.

Above right: Theatrical impresario and Showman, John Hollingshead (1827-1904), a cartoon by Alfred Bryan.

Left: The Gaiety Theatre interior, 1868. The theatre was located on Aldwych at the eastern end of the Strand. It was damaged by bombing in the Second World War and demolished in 1956.

Trial by Jury

(25 March 1875, 131 performances)

Gilbert finally called on Sullivan and read the libretto to him on 20 February 1875. Sullivan was enthusiastic, later recalling:

> [Gilbert] read it through ... in the manner of a man considerably disappointed with what he had written. As soon as he had come to the last word, he closed up the manuscript violently, apparently unconscious of the fact that he had achieved his purpose so far as I was concerned, inasmuch as I was screaming with laughter the whole time.

Above: A scene from *Trial by Jury* as illustrated in the magazine *Illustrated Sporting and Dramatic News*, 1 May 1875.

Right: Gilbert's original sketch of *Trial by Jury*, published in *Fun*, 11 April 1868.

Left: W. S. Gilbert's illustration for 'Now, Jurymen, hear my advice'.

Right: W. S. Gilbert's illustration for 'So I fell in love with a rich attorney's Elderly, ugly daughter'.

The Sorcerer

(17 November 1877, 178 performances)

According to the critic for *The Times* and *The Era* respectively:

[The Sorcerer] achieved a genuine success, and, moreover, a success in every respect deserved.… the libretto, both in the prose and poetical portions, displays remarkable facility in writing fanciful and witty dialogue; and the lively flow of Mr. Sullivan's music, always tuneful, bright, and sparkling, and frequently reaching a very high standard of excellence, could hardly fail to please.

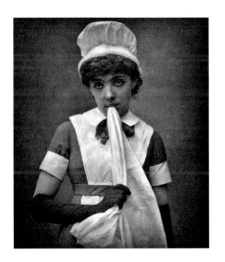

Above left: Jessie Bond as Constance in *The Sorcerer*. Photograph by Herbert Rose Barraud, 1885.

Jessie Charlotte Bond (1853-1942) was best known for creating the mezzo-soprano soubrette roles in the Gilbert and Sullivan operas. She spent twenty years on the stage, the bulk of them with the D'Oyly Carte Opera Company.

Above right: The incantation scene.

Left: Drawing of the title character in *The Sorcerer*, from *Songs of a Savoyard*, by W. S. Gilbert, 1890.

H.M.S. Pinafore

(25 May 1878, 571 performances)

The critic for *The Era* wrote:

> Seldom indeed have we been in the company of a more joyous audience.... [Gilbert and Sullivan] have on previous occasions been productive of such legitimate amusement, such novel forms of drollery, such original wit, and unexpected whimsicality, that nothing was more natural than for the audience to anticipate an evening of thorough enjoyment. The expectation was fulfilled completely.

Above: An illustration of a scene from *H.M.S. Pinafore* from the original theatre poster and playbill created for the original production in 1878 at the Opera Comique, London.

Far left: A woodblock-print advertisement for an 1879 American production of *H.M.S. Pinafore*. *Library of Congress*

Near left: Jessie Bond as Hebe with George Grossmith as Sir Joseph. A photograph from the 1887 revival.

The Pirates of Penzance

(31 December 1879, New York, 3 April 1980, London, 363 performances)

The critic for *The Graphic* wrote:

> … One might fancy that verse and music were of simultaneous growth, so closely and firmly are they interwoven. Away from this consideration, the score of The Pirates of Penzance is one upon which Mr. Sullivan must have bestowed earnest consideration, for independently of its constant flow of melody, it is written throughout for voices and instruments with infinite care, and the issue is a cabinet miniature of exquisitely defined proportions … a brilliant success.

The Pirate Publisher—An International Burlesque that has the Longest Run on Record by Joseph Ferdinand Keppler, published as a centrefold in US magazine *Puck*, 24 February 1886. A commentary on the state of US copyright laws that, prior to a 1911 treaty, generally offered no protection to foreign authors and works.

Far left: W. S. Gilbert's 'Bab' drawing of the modern major-general, *c.* 1880.

Near left: A studio photograph by Herbert Rose Barraud of Richard Temple as the Pirate King and George Grossmith as Major-General Stanley.

117

Patience
(23 April 1881, 578 performances)

According to Gilbert's biographer Edith Browne, the title character, Patience, was made up and costumed to resemble the subject of a Luke Fildes painting. *Patience* was not the first satire of the aesthetic movement played by Richard D'Oyly Carte's Opera Company at the Opera Comique. Grossmith himself had written a sketch in 1876 called *Cups and Saucers* that was revived as a companion piece to *H.M.S. Pinafore* in 1878, which was a satire of the blue pottery craze.

Above: 1885 Programme of a private performance of the second act of *Patience* which took place in W. S. Gilbert's home in 1885.

Far left: Lillian Russell as Patience at the Bijou Opera House in New York, 1882.

Near left: An unidentified actor playing the part of Reginald Bunthorne. This is a contemporary photograph to the early 1880s and was probably a performer in one of several of Richard D'Oyley Carte's companies touring the provinces.

Iolanthe

(25 November 1882, 398 performances)

At the time they wrote *Iolanthe*, both Gilbert and Sullivan were in their peak creative years, and Iolanthe, their seventh work together, drew the best from both composer and author. Sullivan's biographer, Arthur Jacobs, wrote: '[Sullivan] had composed a brilliant new score (his most subtle yet) to a scintillating libretto. ... *Iolanthe* is the work in which Sullivan's operetta style takes a definite step forward, and metamorphosis of musical themes is its characteristic new feature. ... By recurrence and metamorphosis of themes Sullivan made the score more fluid'.

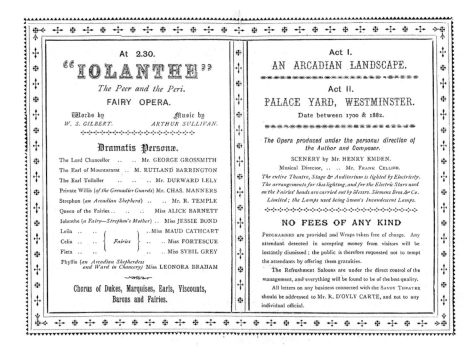

At 2.30.

"IOLANTHE"

The Peer and the Peri.

FAIRY OPERA.

Words by	Music by
W. S. GILBERT.	ARTHUR SULLIVAN.

Dramatis Personæ.

The Lord Chancellor .. .. .. Mr. GEORGE GROSSMITH.
The Earl of Mountararat .. M. RUTLAND BARRINGTON.
The Earl Tolloller .. .. .. Mr. DURWARD LELY.
Private Willis (*of the Grenadier Guards*) Mr. CHAS. MANNERS.
Strephon (*an Arcadian Shepherd*) .. .. Mr. R. TEMPLE.
Queen of the Fairies .. .. .. Miss ALICE BARNETT.
Iolanthe (*a Fairy—Strephon's Mother*) .. Miss JESSIE BOND.
Leila .. ..Miss MAUD CATHCART
Celia .. .. { *Fairies* } .. .. Miss FORTESCUE
Fleta .. .. Miss SYBIL GREY
Phyllis (*an Arcadian Shepherdess and Ward in Chancery*) Miss LEONORA BRAHAM

Chorus of Dukes, Marquises, Earls, Viscounts, Barons and Fairies.

Act I.

AN ARCADIAN LANDSCAPE.

Act II.

PALACE YARD, WESTMINSTER.

Date between 1700 & 1882.

The Opera produced under the personal direction of the Author and Composer.

SCENERY by Mr. HENRY EMDEN.

Musical Director, ... Mr. FRANK CELLIER.

The entire Theatre, Stage & Auditorium is lighted by Electricity. The arrangements for this lighting, and for the Electric Stars used on the Fairies' heads are carried out by Messrs. Siemens Bros. & Co. Limited; the Lamps used being Swan's Incandescent Lamps.

NO FEES OF ANY KIND

PROGRAMMES are provided and Wraps taken free of charge. Any attendant detected in accepting money from visitors will be instantly dismissed ; the public is therefore requested not to tempt the attendants by offering them gratuities.

The Refreshment Saloons are under the direct control of the management, and everything will be found to be of the best quality.

All letters on any business connected with the SAVOY THEATRE should be addressed to Mr. R. D'OYLY CARTE, and not to any individual official.

Above: The inside of the programme from the original run of Gilbert and Sullivan's *Iolanthe*, 1882.

Near right: George Grossmith as The Lord Chancellor in *Iolanthe*.

Far right: Rutland Barrington (1853-1922) as the Earl of Mountararat in *Iolanthe*. A studio photograph by Elliott and Fry, Baker Street, London.

Princess Ida

(5 January 1884, 246 performances)

The reviewer for *The Sunday Times* wrote that the score of Ida was 'the best in every way that Sir Arthur Sullivan has produced, apart from his serious works.... Humour is almost as strong a point with Sir Arthur... as with his clever collaborator....' The humour of the piece also drew the comment that Gilbert and Sullivan's work 'has the great merit of putting everyone in a good temper'. The praise for Sullivan's effort was unanimous, though Gilbert's work received some mixed notices.

Left: Page 2 of original Savoy Theatre programme, May 1884, for *Princess Ida*.

Right: The opera satirises feminism, women's education and Darwinian evolution. A cartoon from *Fun*, 16 November 1872, a caricature of Charles Darwin.

Left: Jessie Bond as Princess Ida.

Right: W. Russell Flint illustration, 1909: luncheon scene Act II: Hilarion (disguised as a woman) speaks with Ida.

The Mikado

(14 March 1885, 672 performances)

Leslie Baily, writing in his 1952 book *The Gilbert & Sullivan Book* refers to Gilbert striding up and down his library in the new house at Harrington Gardens, fuming at the impasse with Sullivan on a suitable topic, when a huge Japanese sword decorating the wall fell with a clatter to the floor. Gilbert picked it up. His perambulations stopped. 'It suggested the broad idea', as he said later. Gilbert had seen the little Japanese men and women from the Exhibition shuffling in their exotic robes through the streets of Knightsbridge. Now he sat at his writing desk and picked up his pen.

Left: Theatre poster, Edinburgh, 1885. The Royal Lyceum Theatre is a 658-seat theatre in Edinburgh, built in 1883. Sybil Grey as Peep-Bo, Leonora Braham as Yum-Yum and Jessie Bond as Pitti-Sing—the three sisters, wards of Ko-Ko.

Right: George Grossmith, as Ko-Ko in *The Mikado*, 1885.

Left: Geraldine Ulmar (1862-1932), Yum-Yum in the New York cast.

Right: Rutland Barrington as Pooh-Bah, Lord High Everything-else.

Ruddigore

(22 January 1887, 288 performances)

The first night was not a success, as critics and the audience felt that *Ruddigore* did not measure up to its predecessor, *The Mikado*. After some changes it achieved a run of 288 performances. The piece was profitable, and the reviews were not all bad. *The Illustrated London News* praised the work of both Gilbert and, especially, Sullivan:

> Sir Arthur Sullivan has eminently succeeded alike in the expression of refined sentiment and comic humour. In the former respect, the charm of graceful melody prevails; while, in the latter, the music of the most grotesque situations is redolent of fun.

Left: The ghost scene, depicted by H. M. Brock for the first D'Oyly Carte Opera Company revival in 1921, at The Price's Theatre, published in *The Sphere*, 29 October 1921.

Right: Jessie Bond as Mad Margaret.

Far left: Another photo of Courtice Pounds as Richard Dauntless in *Ruddigore*, this time a London production.

Near left: Ruddigore poster for the Royal Lyceum Theatre, Edinburgh, 1887.

The Yeomen of the Guard

(30 October 1888, 423 performances)

As opening night approached, Gilbert became increasingly apprehensive. Would the audience accept this serious, sentimental tone from one of the duo's 'comic' operas? Gilbert, always nervous himself on opening nights, came backstage before the performance on opening night to 'have a word' with some of the actors, inadvertently conveying his worries to the cast. Jessie Bond, who was to open the show with a solo song alone on stage, finally said to him, 'For Heaven's sake, Mr Gilbert, go away and leave me alone, or I shan't be able to sing a note!'.

Left: W. H. Denny (1853-1915), born William Henry Leigh Dugmore, was a baritone in the D'Oyly Carte Opera Company. Photographed here with Jessie Bond in *The Yeomen of the Guard*, 1888.

Right: W. H. Denny in *The Yeomen of the Guard*, a caricature by Alfred Bryan in the *Entr'acte Annual*, 1889.

Left: The Yeomen of the Guard poster by illustrator and painter Dudley Hardy (1867-1922).

Right: George Grossmith as Jack Point in *The Yeomen of the Guard*, 1888. A studio photograph by Herbert Rose Barraud, Oxford Street, London

The Gondoliers

(7 December 1889, 544 performances)

The Illustrated London News reported:

Mr. W. S. Gilbert has returned to the Gilbert of the past, and everyone is delighted. He is himself again. The Gilbert of *The Bab Ballads*, the Gilbert of whimsical conceit, inoffensive cynicism, subtle satire, and playful paradox; the Gilbert who invented a school of his own, who in it was schoolmaster and pupil, who has never taught anybody but himself, and is never likely to have any imitator—this is the Gilbert the public want to see, and this is the Gilbert who on Saturday night was cheered till the audience was weary of cheering any more.

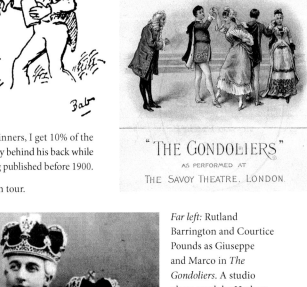

Above: 'At charity dinners, the best of speech-spinners, I get 10% of the takings!' The Duke of Plaza-Toro accepting money behind his back while standing at a dinner table. A Gilbert 'Bab' drawing published before 1900.

Right: 1890 advertisement for *The Gondoliers* on tour.

Far left: Rutland Barrington and Courtice Pounds as Giuseppe and Marco in *The Gondoliers*. A studio photograph by Herbert Rose Barraud, Oxford Street, London.

Near left: Wallace Brownlow (1861-1919), a baritone, and Decima Moore (1871-1964), soprano, born as Lilian Decima Moore, as Luiz and Casilda in *The Gondoliers*, 1889.

Utopia Limited

(7 October 1893, 245 performances)

The Savoy audiences were glad to see Gilbert and Sullivan back together, and the first-night reception was rapturous. Sullivan wrote in his diary:

> Went into the orchestra at 8.15 sharp. My ovation lasted 65 seconds! Piece went wonderfully well—not a hitch of any kind, and afterwards G. and I had a double call.

The critics were divided on the merits of the piece. *Punch*, habitually hostile to Gilbert, commented, '"Limited" it is, in more senses than one'. *The Standard*, by contrast, said, 'Mr. Gilbert and Sir Arthur Sullivan are here at their very best ...'

An early advertisement for an American performance showing the Drawing Room Scene. *Library of Congress*

W. S. Gilbert reading *Utopia (Limited)* to the Actors at the Savoy Theatre. An illustration from *The Savoy Opera* by Percy Fitzgerald, 1894.

The Grand Duke
(7 March 1896, 123 performances)

The Grand Duke is longer than most of the earlier Gilbert and Sullivan operas, and more of the libretto is devoted to dialogue. Gilbert's cutting of parts of the opera after the opening night did not prevent it from having a shorter run than any of the earlier collaborations. In addition to whatever weaknesses the show had, the taste of the London theatre-going public had shifted away from comic opera to musical comedies. One of the most successful musical comedies of the 1890s, *The Geisha* (1896), competed directly against *The Grand Duke* and was by far the greater success.

Left: The Grand Duke poster by illustrator and painter Dudley Hardy (1867-1922).

Centre: Ilka Pálmay (1859-1945), born Ilona Petráss, was a Hungarian-born singer and actress. In 1895, Pálmay began to perform in London, and in 1896 she created the leading role of Julia Jellicoe in *The Grand Duke*. In 1897, Palmay returned to Hungary and spent most of the rest of her long and successful career in Hungary and Austria. She continued to perform until 1928.

Right: Walter [Henry] Passmore (1867-1946), was the first successor to George Grossmith in the baritone roles with the D'Oyly Carte Opera Company. Passmore joined the D'Oyly Carte Opera Company in 1893. He created the role of Grand Duke Rudolph in *The Grand Duke*. A studio photograph by Ellis and Walery.

Far left: Rutland Barrington and Ilka Pálmay in *The Grand Duke*, 1896.

Near left: Charles Kenningham (1860-1925), joined the Doyly Carte Opera Company in 1891 as a tenor, here as Ernest in *The Grand Duke*, 1896.